HOLDING ONTO AIR

HOLDING ONTO AIR

The Art and Science
of Building a Resilient Spirit

Michele DeMarco, PhD

BK
Berrett–Koehler Publishers, Inc.

Berrett-Koehler Publishers, Inc.
1333 Broadway, Suite 1000
Oakland, CA 94612-1921
Tel: (510) 817-2277
Fax: (510) 817-2278
www.bkconnection.com

Ordering Information

Quantity sales. Special discounts are available on quantity purchases by corporations, associations, and others. For details, contact the "Special Sales Department" at the Berrett-Koehler address above.

Individual sales. Berrett-Koehler publications are available through most bookstores. They can also be ordered directly from Berrett-Koehler:
Tel: (800) 929-2929; Fax: (802) 864-7626; www.bkconnection.com.

Orders for college textbook/course adoption use. Please contact Berrett-Koehler:
Tel: (800) 929-2929; Fax: (802) 864-7626.

Distributed to the U.S. trade and internationally by Penguin Random House Publisher Services.

Berrett-Koehler and the BK logo are registered trademarks of Berrett-Koehler Publishers, Inc.

Printed in the United States of America

Berrett-Koehler books are printed on long-lasting acid-free paper. When it is available, we choose paper that has been manufactured by environmentally responsible processes. These may include using trees grown in sustainable forests, incorporating recycled paper, minimizing chlorine in bleaching, or recycling the energy produced at the paper mill.

Library of Congress Cataloging-in-Publication Data

Names: DeMarco, Michele, author.
Title: Holding onto air : the art and science of building a resilient spirit / Michele
    DeMarco, PhD.
Description: First edition. | Oakland, CA : Berrett-Koehler Publishers, Inc., [2024] |
    Includes bibliographical references and index.
Identifiers: LCCN 2023026698 (print) | LCCN 2023026699 (ebook) | ISBN 9781523004874
    (paperback) | ISBN 9781523004881 (pdf) | ISBN 9781523004898 (epub) |
    ISBN 9781523004904 (audio)
Subjects: LCSH: Resilience (Personality trait) | Grief.
Classification: LCC BF698.35.R47 D463 2024 (print) | LCC BF698.35.R47 (ebook) |
    DDC 155.2/4—dc23/eng/20230912
LC record available at https://lccn.loc.gov/2023026698
LC ebook record available at https://lccn.loc.gov/2023026699

First Edition

30 29 28 27 26 25 24 23   10 9 8 7 6 5 4 3 2 1

Book production: Linda Jupiter, Jupiter Productions
Cover design: Ashley Ingram and Michele DeMarco
Cover photo: Max Bender
Text design: Kim Scott, Bumpy Design
Edit: Susan Gall
Proofread: Mary Kanable
Index: Mary Ann Lieser

For my parents,
whose enduring love and support
gives wings to my own resilient spirit.

We cannot re-create our lives going backward.
We can only reclaim our life moving forward.

—MICHELE DEMARCO

CONTENTS

AUTHOR'S NOTE

Hi, I'm Michele, and I'm honored you're here. I'm also sorry you need to be if you or someone you love is dealing with what can only be described as one of the most challenging or soul-sucking times in your (or their) life. But here you are—and here is where you must be because *Holding onto Air* is truly where the path to healing and sustainable wellness begin.

Let me tell you why—and earn your trust.

This book has been a long time in the making—two decades to be specific, back to my early days studying world religion and philosophy, comparative culture and conflict, and psychology and relational therapy. It started out as a bold little handbook for grief and loss—something to overcome the tendency of many "self-help" books to offer merely rudimentary maps for navigating grief and loss's rocky terrain, with tired tropes and shop-worn strategies, often about "being positive" and "thinking happy thoughts." Same old, same old in different language and a pretty cover. As a therapist, clinical ethicist, and trauma researcher, I am more than aware that innocence, once lost, cannot be recovered, and no simple platitude can will that away.

Yes, I said *innocence.* Let me be clear, when you've lost something meaningful—whether that is a loved one or friend, pet, your health, security, job, finances, relationship, faith, trust, moral compass, dignity, an opportunity, and so on—you've not only lost the thing itself, but also *a part of yourself*, your innocence. There is lots more to say on this subject in the following pages, but herein lies one of the key differences between this book and others: *Holding onto Air* is the first book to illuminate the *dual nature of loss*—the science behind it and the art of transforming it.

I wrote this book for people like you, whose worlds have been turned upside down and few things make sense, and you feel as though you're drowning in a vast sea of suckitude, calling into question, well, most things that you've come to rely on. It's for those facing the initial, dizzying, "wtf?!" days of loss or despair or for those stuck in the interminable, wearisome limbo of not knowing how to move forward. It's also for people whose experience of lost innocence occurred in the more distant past, who have yet to fully reconcile it. In other words, *Holding onto Air* is for everyone who knows the pain of lost innocence.

Here is what you'll get and can expect.

Holding onto Air offers a unique and trusted guide for the essential journey of reclaiming your life in the face of lost innocence and building a resilient spirit. Through rigorous research, poignant narratives, and a painstakingly developed framework that includes step-by-step instruction, exercises, mindfulness-based practices, life tips, writing/journaling, and creative inspiration, you will learn how to see yourself in the fullness of time (or as I refer to it a "coherent sense of time") and integrate all your experiences to *Honor the Past, Transform the Present*, and *Craft a New Story for the Future* (HTC—the name of the framework in this book).

Here's what you *won't* get in *Holding onto Air*:

"Beat the grief" philosophies and approaches to healing. Building a resilient spirit isn't about performing better and motivating yourself more, or learning to collaborate better, as some folks would have you believe. In fact, these business-based positive psychology strategies for trauma, grief, and loss fly in the face of emotion science, which overwhelmingly shows that clobbering difficult emotions and feelings that emerge with rational analyses or artificial meaning serves only to delegitimize them, and this ensures that they never fully metabolize, which prevents people from fully healing.

Although *Holding onto Air* has a very clear-sighted approach to lost innocence, it does so with "benevolent honesty," a phrase I coined to describe a kind of clear-eyed, no-rose-colored glasses, no blinders, no exaggeration way to engage with challenge or loss, but to do so with kindness and compassion—a gentleness with ourselves and others as we absorb new realities. This ensures that feelings of rage, bitterness, and resentment don't become emboldened.

Pathologizing or problematizing lost innocence. Whereas some folks (and books) see grief, loss, and trauma as a disorder or a problem to be solved, I (and *Holding onto Air*), view such experiences as natural human struggles to be integrated for good and leveraged for growth. I challenge certain conventional wisdom about the nature of suffering and normalize the experience of grief and despair, taking it out of the world of pathology and problem, as well as the rigid, universalized healing timetables.

"Moral of the story" or "Making lemons out of lemonade" mantras. As I mentioned, there is simply no getting around the fact that meaningful loss, especially the loss of innocence, is absolute, irreducible, and irreplaceable. And no simple cliché, however well-intended, can will it away. This said, *Holding onto Air* does suggest that within every experience throughout our lives, including the loss of innocence, there are "kernel of truths," that is messages, meanings, or insights that are inherently worthy, and therefore worth carrying with you and even inspiring you going forward.

The "H" in the "HTC" framework (*Honor the Past*) shows you specifically how to find these kernels and use them for good.

Ranking grief and loss. I've heard it suggested that some grief is more worthy than other grief, such as the loss of pets, parents, and grandparents are less worthy than a spouse or child. Similarly, that loss derived from beyond the natural order of things (e.g., natural disasters, man-made disasters, accidents and illnesses, violent crimes, and suicides) is more worthy of prolonged grief than other grief. As someone who has worked in a clinical capacity with people who have experienced grief and loss in the aforementioned categories, and who has personally experienced the same, respectfully, I would suggest it is the meaning of loss to an individual that determines the intensity of experience, in addition to their attachment styles and previous experience with trauma—not how nonhierarchal, non-normative, or unnatural it is, as much research shows.

Well-intentioned, but ultimately self-defeatist "wisdom." There have been attempts to disavow the positive psychology "you-can-overcome" approaches to grief and loss by arguing for a more stoic approach, such as "moving on" is a myth or feeling comfort again is an illusion. Although it's true that we can never regain certain aspects of our innocence, viewing grief as a permanent state runs the risk of seeing yourself as eternally damaged. I'm an ardent believer that the same life that brings us joy also (sometimes) brings us pain. More importantly, I affirm that every aspect of life has a role to play in making us who we are today and who we'll be tomorrow. What's important is integrating these experiences into the narratives we live by. We don't always have control over the events in life, but the script we live by is ours to write—and write it we must, as only we can.

Speaking to you from on high. More than a simple self-help "how-to," written by a disconnected academic or detached clinician, I also offer my own story of lost innocence that, at thirty-three years old, unexpectedly, forced me to walk along the knife-edge of life—quite literally. Against the odds, I survived several unexpected close calls with death having to do in various ways with my health. I can tell you that my life for some time was like living inside a washing machine on the tumble and spin cycles. Even today, more than a decade later, I still live with the mystery of why these events happened and with a degree of uncertainty about the future—I suppose as we all do, in the big picture.

My story of lost innocence—both its struggles and successes, as they are—are shared in snippets throughout the book to show how the framework works in practice. This framework was developed prior to these events, reconsidered in light of them, and updated and tested in broader populations in their wake, both through my research and clinical practice. I've been in—and in some ways remain—in the existential trenches with you.

I named this book *Holding onto Air* because grasping for the life we lost, as we do when we lose our innocence, has the same success as trying to clutch the life-giving gas. But even though our hands can't physically grip air, holding onto it and distributing it, through the process of breathing, is precisely what we do at every moment of our lives. In this way, the vital energy of our spirit is like air to our lungs; it fills us up, makes us come alive, and without it we die.

As one of my readers told me, *Holding onto Air* is the book that *none of us* wants on our bedside table or in our digital library, but it's the one that everyone breathes a huge sigh of relief to see when life throws us into a situation that leaves us wholly and existentially "winded."

Honoring the pain of lost innocence, reconciling difficult

truths, transforming ways of thinking and being, and building a resilient spirit starts here and now. All you need to do is turn the page. And know that I'll be there with you at each step. Please note that all uncredited quotes that appear in the book were written by me.

Wishing you peace and wellness.
With gratitude for your interest and trust.

PART 1

Lost Innocence

CHAPTER ONE

WHEN THE UNIMAGINABLE STRIKES

I was thirty-three years old when my greatest fear became a reality, and everything I knew, everything I trusted, both in myself and life, came crashing down around me.

Warning: *Descriptive detail of medical trauma.*

To: Michele's Family and Friends
From: Bill
Date: Tuesday, July 01, 2008, 1:05 AM
Subject: HEART ATTACK!

Dear Everyone,

Thanks for your nice phone calls and messages. I'm home now from Mass General Hospital but beat tired and going to bed. Here are some of the details . . . as few as they are.

It turns out that the pain Michele was having in her chest and back these last few days was a heart attack—for real, no foolin' around. And a pretty bad one at that, as doctors told us. And not the kind they had originally thought—which makes sense given her otherwise good health and that she has no risk factors or family history. What caused hers is apparently really rare. More on that later. The residents were all trying furiously to find something in the medical case literature about the condition. I guess there isn't much—not many people have ever seen it. For a while everyone looked really concerned. I know I am. But she made it through the surgery and is now awake and resting in the CCU. Still, we have no assurances or guarantees.

They've got cardiologists and geneticists and a slew of other medical professionals testing her for everything under the sun. They're desperately trying to figure out why this happened, but so far, they've come up dry. I guess time will tell—or maybe it won't. The doctors all are scratching their heads.

They're cautiously optimistic that with medication and rehab, eventually, she'll be back to her old self, but as she said to me tonight, "I'm not sure who that is anymore."

And therein lies the issue . . .

This was the email that my then husband, Bill, wrote to close family and friends nearly twenty-four hours after I'd almost lost my life. I look at it now all these years later and still wonder, *How was this even possible?* It's the kind of thing you see on television, not the kind of thing you live.

The irony is that I'd spent the entirety of my life intentionally ignoring death. Funerals, no. Horror movies, definitely not. Thoughts of heaven or hell, wasn't going there. For a few years, when I was young, even "Breaking News" sent me fleeing from the television to my private bunker beneath the stairs, where a Strawberry Shortcake sleeping bag, a few favorite books, some snacks, and a flashlight could delude me into thinking that all would be okay—always.

But then I woke up, quite literally, on the last day of June 2008, feeling as though an elephant was standing on my chest and that I'd been slammed in the back by an assailant with a pipe. And I continued to "stay awake" after an aborted trip to the ER, having convinced myself that the symptoms were all but gone, only to return three days later, blurry eyed and barely able to breathe. And I thought I'd never sleep again after six hours of blood draws, X-rays, CT scans, and MRIs, and an ambulance with me in it, threading the needle through stopped traffic and blowing through red lights at top speed. But when all manner of medical professionals shrugged their shoulders and furrowed their brows, consulting textbooks and colleagues around the globe via phone, convinced for some time that I must be a cocaine addict (despite all evidence to the contrary) because who else at my age and with an otherwise healthy body and healthy heart would be circling the drain with a heart attack, I knew I could never go back to the dream that had been my life.

Something was lost. Something indeterminate had awoken. And something in me had changed forever.

I remember that first night in Mass General Hospital, lying on my back in the CCU, dim, cold light surveilling me from overhead, wires stuck all over my body feeding information, staccato-like, to the monitors beside me. I was supposed to have long been in dreamland, but in the hospital, where you go to rest, nobody sleeps. They wake you too often for that. Every hour a new face would appear—some with paper cups and pills, others with a multitude of questions and a pen. At one point, a group of people clad in white came in and flanked my bed, and the tallest among them began barking out orders as each one poked and prodded me.

I remember the doctor saying the words "heart attack," after he'd just said, "you're having." I actually spun my head around to see who the poor soul was getting the bad news. But *I* was that soul. And the news didn't stop there. I'd had a dissection in a coronary artery for no apparent reason, commonly referred to as SCAD. Then, a week later, I had another one—a worse one that made everyone's face turn increasingly grave. Two heart attacks in one week, and still no one knew why.

I remember lying on the OR table surrounded by a blazing white light and people all in green, with a television monitor suspended over my head and a navy paper screen in front of my face. And then, at one point, hearing lots of commotion and someone leaping up on top of me after another yelled, "We're losing her!"

I remember waiting to be discharged after heart attack number two a week later, having just taken a shower for the first time in a week, wondering what could be taking this process so damn long. And then a newly familiar face appeared in the doorway, and its owner smiled, as he walked in and sat down in the chair across from my bed. Then his eyes bore into mine, as he said the words I never wanted to hear: "You should *not* get pregnant because carrying and birthing a child will likely kill you."

I remember arriving home that afternoon with everything just as I'd left it, yet none of it seemed the same. I thought, *I'm living someone else's life*—certainly this couldn't be mine. Only days before my life had been full of health, hope, and possibility. Now, it was filled with a sense of emptiness and vulnerability I'd never known.

I remember one evening wiping tears from my eyes, as I sat on the sofa in my sunroom surrounded by pillows and nothing sharp. My doctor had just called to relay the bad news that my INR (International Normalized Ratio—a measurement used to determine the effects of anticoagulants on the body's clotting system) was off the charts—again. In other words, the blood thinners I was taking to "maybe" prevent a third attack had, for reasons they also couldn't determine, turned my blood into the consistency of water—which meant that if I cut myself, I could bleed out and die. As I listened in the distance to Bill scraping the knife that I was forbidden to use across the plate where my dinner lay, I saw Rory, my Maine Coon kitty, appear from behind the chair and promenade, with enviable confidence, toward the sliding glass door across the room. Then she flopped in the warmth of the afternoon's glow—as if the world hadn't just imploded and all was still okay.

And that's when I realized I was no longer like her—an innocent house cat with her tail raised high, swaggering naively in the sun, but rather a fearfully feral being, hiding alone and uncertain in the shadows of life's dark realities.

My grandmother used to say, "The things you worry about most rarely happen." Whether that's true or not, things *do* happen—painful things, unimaginable things, things that make you call into question beliefs you've always held dear and values that have grounded and guided you, things that leave you with a hole in your heart, aching for what was, despairing for what is, and anxious about what will be, and who *you* will be—*now.*

If you're reading this book, perhaps you, or someone you know, have experienced this kind of thing. And if you are, I can only say, you're not alone. Although it may sound cliché, it's also the truth. Suffering and loss, challenge and crises are unavoidable parts of the human condition. None of us can avoid heartache. None of us can hold onto our carefree, childlike innocence forever. Life simply doesn't work that way. Therefore, the very real experience of lost innocence is universal—it happens to each of us, and often when we least expect it. It happens when someone lets us down or betrays us, or when we betray our own conscience or moral compass. It happens when a meaningful belief is called into question or when our certainty is challenged. It happens when we lose a loved one, either to death or because a meaningful relationship has ended. It happens when we are given an unwelcome diagnosis, or when we lose our job, or when our children are heading in a direction that concerns us. It happens anytime some distressing or traumatic event occurs in either our individual or collective life. And it happens in our own private anxieties when we encounter the core mysteries of existence. Simply speaking, lost innocence happens just from being human and from being alive. In fact, it's the price we pay for life.

But here's another truth: We don't survive *despite* challenge or loss; we flourish *because of* them. We don't build resilience by trying to "get back" or "go back" to what was, nor by simply "thinking happy thoughts" for now. We do it by honoring and integrating *all* our experience—past, present, and future—into the fullness of life and into the fullness of our being. It's true: losing something meaningful, such as our innocence, may be painful and dislocating. It may leave us restless and confused. It may paralyze our good sense and our ability to move forward. It may even darken our spirit— for a time. But as I have learned, through both bitter and wonderful experience, it is also the starting point for an empowered and well-lived life. In fact, it can be our greatest existential (or human) "return on investment"—that is, *if* we allow it to be.

I admit that in the weeks and months after my heart attacks my spirit wasn't well. First there was surgery and recovery and all manner of medication (one of which turned me into a walking bruise), skipped and erratic heartbeats, the occasional stabbing pains in my chest, a racing and sometimes pounding heart, and an irksome "tugging" in my upper left arm. Add to this ongoing fatigue, sleeplessness, lightheadedness, and occasional short-lived anxiety and the lack of available information on my condition, the uncertainty as to whether it would happen again, *and* the news of no getting pregnant even though that had been the plan (*sigh*) ... I truly didn't know which way was up. I remember ambling around as if in a fog, mired in confusion, occasionally paralyzed by fear, lacking confidence and a compass to show me the way forward.

And I was angry—not necessarily at life or God or fate for "allowing" this to happen. Rather, at myself, because I shouldn't have felt this way—or so I thought. I'd spent the last decade of my life immersed in the world of "spirit wellness" and resilience. I was the last person who should have been feeling this way.

Sometime in the early days of our new millennium, I decided to go back to school to study theology. My announcement shocked everyone, including me. I was the child who at twelve years old pitched a fit outside the front door of my religious education classroom demanding to be allowed to drop out of the program that I found to be utterly uninspiring. As a young adult, religion was not a driving influence in my life. But the existential questions that the broad tent of religion and spirituality speak to, and the fundamental human desires that all the great traditions help people to satisfy, each in their own way, have always mattered to me; in fact, they fascinated me from the time I was a young.

I can't pinpoint the moment when I realized what the strong appeal was for me to study theology—so much for having any big epiphany—but sometime between no degrees and three degrees later I came to understand: nowhere does the "funk of living" (to quote the philosopher Cornel West)—the here-and-now, harsh realities of humanity's struggle to live in a world that so easily toggles between tragedy and comedy—become as apparent as it does in the study of religion. Nowhere seems to capture in such raw and compelling narrative our collective desire for hope and healing in the midst of pain and suffering like the various sacred scriptures or the ways in which countless scholars and everyday people grapple with them. Nowhere can the presence of life walk alongside the certainty of death with such profundity as it does in the beliefs and principles, rituals and practices, and identity and community of the world's wisdom traditions.

When you study religion, you are exploring nothing less than the human condition in all its perfect imperfection. Somehow this "funk" is where I found my home. And developing strategies that help people to not only live with that funk but also embrace it, and then because of it, build what I like to think of as a "sustainable spirit," became my life's project.

But then I personally felt the "funk" in the form of two rare heart attacks that left everyone guessing. And so, I was forced to look at and engage this so-called life project in an entirely new way.

Holding onto Air is the result of that effort. Leveraging more than a decade of experience, research, and practice, the following pages offer a fresh approach to dealing with adversity and building that "sustainable spirit"—one that will help you to endure and evolve in the wake of any of life's challenges. More than a simple self-help "how-to," I also offer my own story—both its struggles and successes, as they are—of putting that framework into practice. It wasn't always easy, I'll be honest. In fact, the process has been a good reminder that resilience isn't an end point to achieve but rather something to be lived intentionally, every day. Even now, all these years later, I'm still working to live it.

How do you carry on when happiness, hope, and harmony seem to be taken away? How do you endure when life pushes you to the limits of "you"? How do you move from having a hole in your heart to being whole in spirit? These are life's greatest challenges—and its greatest rewards.

So, I invite you on a journey. Heartache and loss leave you standing at a fork in the road. Together, we'll explore two paths ahead: one that undermines your ability to heal and move forward because it leads you to wallow in what was, be dispirited about what is, and ignore what still can be, and another that leverages your innate capacity for resilience and helps you to hold onto that life-giving air that moves energy through your body, calms your mind, and allows your spirit to soar. In doing so, it will help you to, as a poem I once wrote said, "Transform to triumph . . . renew, not retreat. Rise, from out of chaos and loss comes life."

The following pages will show you how.

But before we do . . .

A word about "spirit" because I know it can sometimes be contentious.

Like an idea, an opinion, a personality, or a dream, *everyone* has spirit. Simply speaking, spirit is the animating energy at the core of our lives. Its expression can be, but does not have to be, dependent on an explicit belief system. So, whether you consider yourself to be a devout believer, a seeker, an atheist, or something else; whether you find "it" in plazas or sanctuaries, a mosque, or a temple, or in communion or in solitude; whether you believe it is part of you or you are part of it; and wherever and however you choose to express it, spirit is part of who you are, and it plays an essential role in whether you are well and able to flourish.

There is much more to say on the subject of spirit, but that's for a different book. Why it's important for this book is for one simple reason: because unlike the body and mind, spirit doesn't diminish with time. It only deepens, grows, and, if allowed to, flourishes in *all* circumstances, including, and especially, tough times.

CHAPTER TWO

LETTING GO OF INNOCENT ASSUMPTIONS

I remember, in no particular order:

One: sitting cross-legged on the red shag carpet in my bedroom, holding a Strawberry Shortcake figurine on the top floor of my dollhouse. My mother appeared in the doorway to give me the news that we were going to visit my beloved grandmother in Pennsylvania. "We are!" I squealed, my heart soaring. "Yes," my mom said, "and we're going to take an airplane!"

Two: standing at a bright wall of glass, me perched on my mother's hip, her pointing to the sky as a jet the size of a dinosaur soared up and disappeared into the clouds. Then, a moment later, another dinosaur wiggled closely above the tarmac, then dropped down onto the runway with a thud and a roar. "See," my mother said, giving me a big hug. "Airplanes go up and they come down. There's nothing to be scared of."

Three: sitting squashed in the window seat of a Boeing 737 beside a man with forearms the size of my head. I was on my way to Disney World to meet my mother for a girl's vacation in anticipation of my high school graduation. She was already in the Magic Kingdom for a professional conference. It was the first time in my life I was absent a flying companion. "Airplanes go up and they come down," I repeated as the jet rolled backward and began to pivot. "There's nothing to be afraid of."

Four: Being 36,000 feet above the ground, with sun streaming in, my Walkman blasting music through my headset, watching out the window as clouds danced around the plane. *How could anything this beautiful be scary?* I thought to myself, relaxing into the seat, with a sense of wonder and calm blanketing me.

Five: Opening the front door and hearing the phone ringing a decade later. Saying "Hello?"; then handing the receiver to my then husband Bill when the faceless voice asked to speak to him. Hearing my ex say, "Hey man! How are you do . . ."; then watching his six-foot-two-inch frame fall slowly toward the floor. Then, hastily throwing a nearby kitchen chair beneath him, as he held the phone away from his ear and said with robotic affect, as he hit the cushion, "He's telling me my brother was on the Alaska Airlines flight that crashed into the Pacific Ocean today, off the coast of Los Angeles."

Six: Sitting in an anodyne hotel ballroom, at one of thirty or forty haphazardly placed tables, surrounded by my ex-husband's grieving family, with eighty-seven other distraught families in close proximity. In the distance, at the front of the room, a man in a navy fleece jacket with white hair stood at a podium, speaking carefully into a staticky microphone about the need for family DNA samples, "for identification purposes," and a forthcoming briefing from National Transportation Safety Board (NTSB) officials, who could answer questions about "aerodynamics and the impact of the crash on the human body."

Planes really do *fall out of the sky*, I thought blankly.

WHAT DOES IT MEAN
TO LOSE OUR INNOCENCE?

One of life's greatest ironies is that we spend our childhood waiting to be adults and our adulthood trying to recapture that childlike innocence. When we're young, we yearn for the secret code that unlocks the forbidden door that only grown-ups can access. But as adults, having witnessed in any number of ways the mysteries that lie behind that door, we sometimes wish we had never found or been given the key. Only in hindsight can we realize that to know or have experienced less is often much easier (and less painful) than to know or have experienced more.

LOST INNOCENCE IS A DUAL LOSS

Whenever we lose something, we actually lose two things. For instance, if we lose our keys, we also lose some time and peace of mind while we try to find or replace them. Or, if we lose our favorite sunglasses or watch, we also lose the money we spent on them, as well as a little "face" because we feel embarrassed that we carelessly left them somewhere unintended. But when we lose something meaningful, something that is very dear to us—like a loved one or friend, our health, security, job, finances, relationship, moral compass, dignity, faith, an opportunity, and so on—not only do we lose the person or thing itself, but also we lose *a part of our self*: our innocence.

Lost innocence is the chipping away of some precious ideal or principle, the crumbling of a certain freedom or confidence and wholeness or integrity, that we have come to rely upon. It's the passing away of a happy ignorance that previously protected us from the painful stuff of life. It is as though we had once been wound contently in bubble wrap and then something pointy popped all the padding.

At its core, lost innocence is a "felt sense" deep inside—one that makes our muscles tighten, our stomach turn, or our heart feel heavy when we suddenly become aware that we, others, even life itself are imperfect and limited—that bad things really do happen to good people, and sometimes for no good reason; that physical pain (such as illness, injury, exhaustion, old age, and eventually death) and emotional suffering (such as fear, frustration, disappointment, and despair) are inescapable parts of life; and that knowledge, as reliable as it can be, is sometimes flawed, so what we and others think we know, we sometimes don't.

CAPTIVES IN A STRANGE NEW WORLD

Tradition reminds us that the loss of innocence is like a rite of passage—an initiation of sorts that is the foundation of mature flourishing. But in the moment, it usually doesn't feel that way.

When adversity happens and steals part of our innocence, we often find ourselves captives in a strange new world, where the familiar still looks the same, but somehow the way we feel about the familiar, and our relationship to it, is suddenly different. It is as if we are alienated from our "normal" world—everyone and everything else is going about life as usual. But for us, "normal" is no more.

Although the disorientation can take its toll on us individually, it can also profoundly affect our relationships. Although friends and loved ones can be sympathetic to our pain and concerned for our well-being, they cannot always understand that though we may look like our usual selves, something meaningful has changed within us. Sometimes it is us who no longer knows how to interact with them anymore. Other times it's them who doesn't know how to approach us. Often, it's both.

I remember in the weeks after my heart attacks I noticed, all too obviously, that the flurry of cards, flowers, and other token well-wishes had come to a halt and that the phone had stopped ringing. And when I did talk to people, they'd often ask, rather reluctantly, "Uh, how are you?" Then they'd nod intently and make sympathetic faces and sounds that, under other circumstances, would be expected and appropriate when I started to fill them in. But their blank stares or no stares, because they were too busy looking at the ground or at the horizon, or else frankly, anywhere other than at me, left me thinking, *Thanks, but you* really *have no idea what I'm talking about, do you*? It was as if I had immigrated to a new world, never to see the old country again.

FEAR OF CHANGE, FEAR OF THE UNKNOWN

The Chinese philosopher Lao Tzu once said, "If you do not change direction, you may end up where you're heading." When lost innocence strikes, we often find ourselves longing for and heading *back* to our innocent past—back to happy days when we didn't know such pain or worry. The problem is we *can't* go back—plain and simple. It's a tough truth to swallow, I know, because the alternative means that we must change direction. Unfortunately, change is not something that comes easy for most people; in fact, many of us seem to naturally want to fight against it. Of course, there's a simple reason: change casts us, like an abandoned stone, from our comfort zones into a vast sea of the unknown. And what we don't know, we can't control. And what we can't control, we often fear.

Let's stop for a moment and look at fear.

Fear sometimes gets a bad rap; it gets confused with weakness or fragility. But fear has an adaptive function: it protects us from danger and helps us to survive. Fear is a basic emotion that is hard-wired into us and other species. As with all emotions, fear is an internal source of information: it communicates impending danger and so allows us to react very quickly to threatening situations by releasing a torrent of hormones that helps us react with haste.

Although a healthy dose of fear can serve its intended purpose, all too easily and too often we allow fear to get the better of us and misdirect, if not commandeer, our lives:

‡ Harmful fear makes us brittle and vulnerable.

‡ Harmful fear makes us expect problems, often for no good reason.

‡ Harmful fear makes us retreat, narrowing our vision, shrinking our horizons, and making us smaller.

‡ Harmful fear paralyzes our good sense and ability to reason well.

‡ Harmful fear makes us cling to things that we think will keep us safe, when in reality they won't.

‡ Harmful fear causes us to lose a sense of meaning— we struggle to make sense of and find significance in anything or anyone.

‡ Harmful fear separates us from our purpose—it distracts us from the things that give us a reason to live.

‡ Harmful fear causes our values to go awry and our relationships to come apart at the seams.

✢ Harmful fear diminishes our ability to be resilient—
and without that, how do we move forward?

Harmful fear prevents us from building a resilient spirit
because it makes our spirit unwell. A life defined by harmful fear
is what I call *The Gray Life*—a blunted, one-dimensional existence
defined by scarcity, separation, and sacrifice. It is a life of "spirit
sickness," and it is no life at all. Here's what I mean:

SPIRIT WELLNESS	SPIRIT SICKNESS
The self is sacred	The self is scared
Full of life	Exhausted by life
You can	You can't and won't
You are	You're not and fear you'll never be
Trust in self	Doubt in self
Have satisfaction	Always craving
Need to "let go"	Need to control
Sense of place	Lost at sea
Clarity of thought	Wishful thinking
Abide in the moment	Fill time
Live with intention	Search for a reason
Settles in	Settles often

Spirit Wellness vs. Spirit Sickness

It's not surprising that lost innocence causes our spirit to be
sick. Not only does adversity change the comfortable rhythm of

our day-to-day lives, but also it changes our comfortable sense of life and our place in it. The problem isn't that our spirit gets sick in these conditions; we all get the occasional cold or flu. Problems occur when we don't treat lost innocence properly or approach healing in the most effective way.

THE PATH FORWARD

So, what do we do to heal our aching heart and our sick spirit when adversity strikes and we lose a part of our innocence? Which way do we turn—because eventually we realize that we *must* change direction? Although the fog of fear and indecision may be thick, eventually two paths appear.

The first path seems easy and painless, like a flat road on an open highway. This path looks as if it will take us directly to where we want to be: *back* to the innocent past. And why wouldn't we want to follow it? It's natural to retreat to something or someplace that we perceive as comfortable, to get back what we once had or to where we once were. Somehow re-creating the past can seem like the best hope for a happy future. But, as we will see, this is the path to nowhere; it merely keeps us in a dispiriting, fear-driven limbo. Memories of yesterday leave our spirit endlessly sick, and abandoned hopes for tomorrow weaken our "spirit immunity," holding us prisoners to our pain. And "now" becomes a narrow place to escape, rather than an expansive opportunity for transformation and engagement. This is the path of *Back and Blue*.

The second path isn't so straightforward or as seemingly safe. In fact, we see that the trail ahead soon curves out of sight toward an unknown destination, like a high mountain pass through an abundant wood. That uncertainty may, at first, cause fear to bubble up, again—because seriously, who in the throes of change and challenge wants to take a chance on the unknown? All we really want just then is to *know* what's coming and to *control* the outcome. And yet if we stay with that uncertainty for a moment longer and listen to what the stirrings deep within are whispering, we see that it's not harmful fear telling us to return to *Back and Blue,* but rather it's our spirit calling us to adventure and beckoning us forward on the path of *Lost and Found.*

For a while, *Back and Blue* seemed to me the obvious choice. But as I came to see, that would have turned me into "a cardiac coward," to quote my no-holds-barred cardiologist, that is someone stuck in the blunted, one-dimensional existence of *The Gray Life.*

The high mountain pass of *Lost and Found* felt a little like summiting Everest, and with a heart in a weakened state, such as mine was, I wasn't sure I had it in me to climb. But its lure was strong, and eventually I found the courage to step onto the path. Quickly, I discovered three clear markers to help me to leverage my spirit, in addition to my body and mind, and navigate the way forward:

1. *Honor the Past*

2. *Transform the Present*

3. *Craft a New Story for the Future*

And so, here we stand at a fork in the road. Let's now explore together the two paths ahead: *Back and Blue* and *Lost and Found,* for this journey will determine whether you are held prisoner to the pain, powerlessness, and uncertainty of lost innocence or truly be freed to live again.

CHAPTER THREE

THE PATH TO NOWHERE: *BACK AND BLUE*

Preserve only that which is right and real for as long as possible,
and have the courage to let go and let be when it is no longer.

BEWARE OF APPEARANCES

Think of a time when something happened in your life that caused you to lose a part of your innocence. Maybe it was an unexpected layoff or not getting an anticipated raise or promotion. Perhaps it was because someone broke up with you or told you they wanted a divorce. Maybe you got the unfortunate news that someone you cared for had a serious medical condition or that you yourself had one. Or perhaps it was that the God you believed in or the workings of the universe let you down. Whatever it was, do you remember how you felt or where you wanted to turn—or turn away from?

When we lose a part of our innocence, instinctually, we seek comfort not chaos, stability not change, and escape not enlightenment. So, it is entirely natural that we would want to get things back to the way they used to be.

Path One, *Back and Blue*, is where we go when we try to re-create who we were, what we had, or how we felt about ourselves, others, or life itself—*before* our challenge or loss. It is our attempt to fill the hole in our heart or quell an internal restlessness by trying to go back "home"—back to happiness, wholeness, and peace.

I mentioned that in the wake of my heart attacks I was told in no uncertain terms that carrying and birthing a child would likely kill me. Not exactly the sentiment you want to hear when you and your partner are entertaining the possibility. The first six months post–heart attacks, I was still adjusting to the new reality of a slew of daily medications, shadow symptoms, doctors' visits, not lifting or carrying anything heavier than fifteen pounds, among a host of other surreal experiences. The subject of adoption or surrogate carriers, then my only safe option, had to be tabled for some time. But despite it all, I was feeling momentum toward having a child. I wanted something more to love and nurture, wanted another pair of eyes and another beating heart in my immediate family. So, I concluded, if not a child now, maybe a dog—specifically, an adopted Greyhound, very apropos, given my situation. In short order, my ex-husband and I were visiting shelters. After two stops, Vito came home with us.

Vito was huge. His back approached my sternum, and he seemed as long as a bus. But Vito was as friendly as could be. The entire ride home, he leaned forward from the back seat and pressed his snout up against my cheek. The big test was going to be whether Vito would chase cats (we had two Maine Coons), and the jury was out. The folks at the rescue center said that the only way to know for sure was to try it out. So, we brought Vito home, where he promptly failed the test. Sadly, most Greyhounds make their living chasing little creatures, real or automated, that move fast. Our cats, catching one glimpse of him, moved like lightning, and he after them. Being limited to lifting only fifteen pounds, I couldn't hold him back. Immediately, the house was in uproar. It took an hour or more before every beating heart in the place calmed to a healthy level. Regrettably, I realized we would have to make Vito available to another, cat-free home.

After a good cry and consulting with the rescue center director on the phone, we drove back and said a sad goodbye to Vito. Then we promptly met Mr. Jay—another grown male Greyhound rumored to be good with cats. So, back to the house he came. This time we kept the cats behind closed doors as we brought Mr. Jay inside. After an hour, he fell asleep with his head on my shoulder; I was smitten. But then suddenly, again, it all went south. I left Mr. Jay alone for literally one minute, and he began howling to raise the roof. That night I slept on the floor beside him, but a trip to the bathroom brought on the wailing once more. When I came back and tried to console him, his seventy pounds of love and neediness knocked me onto my back with him perched on my chest. I finally managed to coax him off, but I panicked all night that the pressure of his weight would cause my precarious coronary arteries to burst open for a third time. But given that I awoke the next morning, not dead, I insisted on taking Mr. Jay for his morning walk—only again, he nearly gave me a heart attack. Proving to be an enthusiastic explorer of new land, it was he who walked (or nearly dragged) me, rather than the other way around. And when we tried to climb the stairs to the back deck of our house, Mr. Jay outright refused. I spent twenty minutes trying to lift his rump up the steps one by one, to no avail. By the time I made it into the house, I was covered in sweat, my blood pressure was through the roof, and I was once again in a pool of tears.

I had to acknowledge that having a dog, let alone a new one, and this one, was just too much. Mr. Jay needed detachment training, gentleness-to-cats training (a bit), housebreaking (this was a very big dog, and Greyhounds apparently don't typically come housebroken), how-to-walk-on-stairs training (apparently, Greyhounds also haven't usually seen stairs), and don't-pull-on-the-leash training, in addition to an electric fence because Mr. Jay would very likely run after critters if we let him off-lead in the backyard, in addition to storing his ginormous bags of food, which I couldn't lift. And, of course, there was the potential that I might never be able to walk him.

I felt like an utter fool and a complete failure. I liked Vito and Mr. Jay, and in time, I know I would have loved them. But in my twisted universe of spirit sickness, my good sense went out the window; it was just too soon and too much. Although I was sad that the pups would not be a part of my family and had every confidence that they would find another loving home, I couldn't stop aching because, in addition to my not being able to bear children, apparently, I couldn't even have a dog. And, at the time, I lived in a town that was brimming with people my age pushing strollers and walking dogs (some even pushing dogs in strollers) and neighbors with cute kids and state-of-the-art jungle gyms. Once again, the alienation from "normal" felt all-encompassing.

Driving home from returning him to the shelter, I felt my heart breaking again. In addition to saying goodbye, this time to Mr. Jay, it felt like saying goodbye to a part of a dream—the life-long plan for that so-called "normal" type of life, complete with a nice house, adorable kids, successful jobs, and fetching dogs, that had unwittingly directed so many of my choices until that moment. Then it occurred to me that I've never really fit into the neat box of "normal" that so many others construct for their lives. *My life, on the whole, really is* never *going to be "normal," is it?* I thought as we drove home absent a soft snout in my ear.

The need for a dog post–heart attacks signified many things, as I eventually came to see: a child to love and feel secure in life, the sense of "normal" that I'd always glimpsed but never had. I was desperate to go back to the dream that filled my life pre–heart attacks, but Vito and Mr. Jay showed me that wasn't possible. I had changed. "Home" had changed. It was like trying to stop myself from falling off a cliff by scrambling to hold onto air.

Back and Blue can never deliver us peace because it cleverly undermines our ability to reconcile pain, heal, and move forward. We start to frame our lives exclusively around painful memories of the past. We live in a lackluster present and live with abandoned hopes for the future. The more we try to grasp what was, the less we feel like there's anything to hold on to. For many people, this suffering eventually becomes something darker and more damaging, as we are about to see.

GRAY TWILIGHT AND FALSE PERSONAS

I am no longer one of them, however. They are up there, on the
face of the earth; I am down here, in the bottom of a well. They
possess the light, while I am in the process of losing it. Sometimes I
feel that I may never find my way back to that world, that I may
never again be able to feel the peace of being enveloped in the light.
... Down here there are no seasons. Not even time exists.

HARUKI MURAKAMI, *THE WIND-UP BIRD CHRONICLE*

Trauma research shows that people who have experienced danger or a threat to their physical lives often experience dissociation; that is, disconnecting from their feelings, thoughts, memories, and identity. These dissociative changes cause alterations in one's sense of time, perception, attentional focus, and awareness of pain. Individuals describe feeling like they lost track of what's going on around them and feeling detached. The sense that time seems to slow down, speed up, or else stop entirely are the most common symptoms of those during or shortly after a traumatic event.

Lost innocence isn't a pathology; rather, it's a human struggle—but there is a spectrum to trauma on which it falls. While lost innocence can result from a threat to a person's life, at its core, lost innocence is more about a threat to the spirit than to the physical body; it is an existential threat or disruption that can also shift how we locate ourselves temporally.

Like a thick, descending, and disorienting fog, when we travel on the path of *Back and Blue*, we often find ourselves wandering in a gray twilight with a distorted sense of space and time that others don't inhabit. "I'm neither here nor there," I remember thinking one day when the acute danger to my life had passed. I was sitting like a lump of clay in a wheelchair pushed by the hospital release attendant. As he held open the car door that was to take me "home" to my new life, it hit me: "I really am *nowhere!*"

Gray Twilight Time

Feeling lost in a fog of nowhere isn't particularly fun. It's *The Gray Life*—that blunted, one-dimensional existence—par excellence. As a species we are adaptive by nature, but because *Back and Blue* offers no relief or sense of "home," we often learn to cope in unhelpful ways. Enter what I call the *Three Ds of The Gray Life*—a recipe for spirit sickness.

DISTRACTION

Friedrich Nietzsche wrote that "haste is universal because everyone is in flight from himself." In the case of lost innocence, nothing could be truer. When the pain of the loss of "what was" gets too overwhelming, diverting our attention often seems like a good thing to do. And it can be for a time; we all need a break from the weight of despair to restore ourselves. But too often that break becomes a way of being, not only because it feels good to feel less bad, which can be addictive, but also because it serves as a way of asserting control in a situation that seemingly stole control from us. The problem is too much distraction keeps us in a disjointed universe with no sense of time and in an incoherent selfhood with no sense of self.

Stop for a moment and read that last sentence again.

Can you think of a time when you felt stuck in a disjointed universe or wanted to "flee yourself"? Better yet, imagine yourself there, sensations and all. Feel what that feeling of being disjointed is doing to you even now. Twitches beneath the surface of your skin? A skipped heartbeat? A tightness or tingle? A wave of overwhelm or fear? A hollowness or helplessness? Over time, these sensations can become learned behavior and negatively affect how we think and act—or distract.

DENIAL

Sigmund Freud first developed the concept of denial as a defense mechanism. He suggested that when painful realities threaten the human ego and make us feel vulnerable, we will often refuse to accept their truth to deal with the emotional conflict. Like distraction, a healthy amount of denial can help us cope; it gives our mind a chance to absorb distressing information in a way that is paced, so that we can take it in and not get overwhelmed. But also, like distraction, denial has a dark side. Pretending something doesn't exist—like whatever caused our loss of innocence—or rejecting realities that occur because of that loss of innocence, only keeps us lost in a menacing fog and in a perpetual state of limbo.

"A perpetual state of limbo"—read that slowly and a few times.

Imagine a situation where you kept ignoring some truth that you didn't like or couldn't accept. Where and how did that truth live inside you? How did it rear its head? And how did you respond? As Freud also pointed out, what we resist, persists.

DISTORTION

Distortion—also known as "cognitive distortion," or what Aaron Beck originally called "selective abstraction," which is now commonly referred to as a "mental filter"—is human beings' tendency to focus on one detail, taken out of context, and ignore other more important parts of an experience. Like distraction and denial, distortion is a manipulation of reality to make an upsetting situation more palatable. Unlike the previous two *D*s, distortion uses pieces of truth to soften the blow—which makes it the most insidious "*D*." Distortion convinces us something isn't *really* true or true in the way it appears. It makes us bend realities that we'd rather not face, to meet our own dreams, wishes, or desires—such as convincing us that we can get back our innocence.

Perhaps you've heard the phrase "keeping up appearances," meaning to pretend everything is good when it is not. Distortion is a bit like that. And it takes a lot of work to keep things "up."

Consider a time when the story you told yourself or others was edited or prettied up to make a situation appear different than it was. Maybe you did it purposely or, in retrospect, you realize now that you did it unknowingly. Put yourself back there in this moment. How much heavy lifting did the distortion require—emotionally, physically? What did it do—or is it doing now—to your body? Do you feel a bit drained or tired? How about your tolerance level: is it perhaps a little shorter? Is there any bitterness bubbling up? If so, you are in very good company.

All *Three Ds of The Gray Life* attempt to block pain from our awareness. But trust me when I say that none are a long-term strategy for peace—the effort to maintain them is simply too great; their weight becomes too much of a burden. There's only so long that we can keep up the pretense of "normal" before something even darker in us shifts.

THE *THREE HARMFUL PERSONAS*

Come in, defeat, come in and make yourself at home.
IRIS MURDOCH, *THE SACRED AND PROFANE LOVE MACHINE*

Many of the world's wisdom traditions celebrate the notion of surrender, that is, stopping the struggle against the things that no longer serve us or the purposeful turning away from all that holds us back, namely harmful fear and ego. Surrender, it's been suggested, is key to a richer, more fulfilled life. But when adversity strikes, and when we're in a tsunami of pain or confusion, and the *Three Ds* no longer serve us as we once thought they might, then often we fall into a state of resignation—which is the opposite of surrender. In both cases, we're giving up or letting go of something, but with surrender it is grounded in trust or faith; with resignation it is mired in having lost something we love. It is the difference between leaning toward something uncertain with hope and retreating from hope thanks to painful realities we now must face.

In the case of lost innocence, when hope is extinguished, we often become a shell of our former selves. To remain whole, we often don what I refer to as one or more of the *Three Harmful Personas*: the numbed-out survivor; the rage and resentment-filled victim; and the misguided martyr. Each persona holds us back. Each persona makes us smaller. And each persona keeps us blue.

Persona One: The Survivor

Many people like to talk about "surviving" after trauma or loss. Given the alternative, it makes good sense. But as I've experienced it, surviving isn't enough because survivors aren't necessarily resilient. To survive means only that you continue to exist after all is said and done. But it is important to remember that there are *many* ways to exist—and not all of them are healthy or serve us well.

The survivor persona allows hardship to feed feelings of fear and disillusionment. We become sullen skins, locked in a prison of haunting discontent or else saturated indifference, both of which tear apart the fabric of our being. We get bored. We act impulsively. We procrastinate. We don't bother. We dwell excessively on our loss, and we fixate on what else we might lose or have taken away.

We think that by "shaking off" adversity, we can detach from the problem or pain. But sadly, this is not the case. In the end, we only prolong the inevitable.

When you think of the survivor persona imagine a zombie or the walking dead. Think of a tarnished penny or a flower that has turned to seed. Think of how food tastes when you have a nasty cold or what things sound like when you have water in your ears. You have survived—but are you really thriving?

Persona Two: The Victim

The victim persona is characterized by a sense of iniquity and blame. When we experience loss, crises, or forced transition, we often feel that we have been wronged, whether it is by someone or something specific or simply by life itself. It's natural to want to know why "this" happened, and especially why "this" happened to us? But in our attempt to demand answers, particularly when they don't come as quickly as we'd like, we can become overly sensitive, easily offended, and sometimes rash.

When we adopt the victim persona, we make ourselves smaller, which only intensifies our suffering. We develop an entitlement mentality and assume a defensive posture. We become consumed by our own feelings and wants at the expense of others. We tend to take more for ourselves and share less with those around us. We struggle to feel empathy and to show compassion. And we become empowered by misplaced anger that has swelled into rage—all of which leads nowhere good.

When you think of the victim persona imagine a captured lion pacing within the small confines of a cage or an aggravated insect slamming against a window, trying to find the freedom of fresh air. Imagine getting stuck in an elevator if you are claustrophobic or being ignored or belittled when you have something important to say. Think of a time when you were bullied or made fun of or abandoned by friends and left helpless to fend for yourself. These are terrible feelings indeed.

When we live as a victim, we allow ourselves to become so identified with our grievance or loss that we stay trapped in a past that only leads to a life of torment. We think that by raging against adversity, we can defeat the problem or make the pain submit. But again, this is not to be. In truth, we only continue to suffer and make our spirit sick.

Persona Three: The Martyr

The martyr complex is well known: the person who seeks sympathy and attention by suffering for the sake of some value or belief; and though many agree it's an unappealing quality, too easily and too often we let the experience of adversity turn us into just this—a martyr.

The martyr persona exploits and contorts our feelings of anguish to such an extent that we willingly commend our life to sacrifice and our spirit to indefinite suffering. As martyrs, no one's pain is ever quite like ours, and no one's response to it is ever noble enough. We demand recognition for what we see as our worthy behavior, and, if it's not forthcoming, or if it is challenged in any way, we often dismiss or break off the relationship with the person who challenged us. Our mistake is that we see virtue in indulging our pain and abstaining from things that could bring us joy. As a result, we forego the possibility of future happiness by relinquishing both our good sense and perspective.

When you think of the martyr persona, imagine an old vinyl record that has reached its end but is now in an eternal loop of static noise, projecting fuzzy, screeching sounds, instead of beautiful music. Think of a tattered blanket or pants that are worn through and beyond repair, whose owner refuses, on principle, to stop wearing them.

The martyr thinks that by wallowing in adversity, they can turn their pain into a crutch to support them and carry them onward. But as with the other two personas, this too gets us nowhere.

THE PATH TO NOWHERE

The Hopi Indians have a saying: "To watch us dance is to hear our hearts speak." So, how does our heart speak when we lose our innocence? For some it might be a deafening cry of rage. For others it is like the eternal drum beat to the gallows. For many, the heart simply loses its voice or freezes with fear, uncertain how to sing again.

Lost innocence of any kind, small or large, anywhere on the traumatic spectrum, can create a hole in our heart and make our spirit sick. This is because it dispels the illusion that life can be perfect, complete, fair, or forever okay. It is the existential restlessness at the heart of the human condition come into stark relief.

Back and Blue is the path to nowhere because it cleverly convinces us that the way to be happy and whole is to get things back to the way they used to be; but unfortunately, as we've seen, this never can be. *Back and Blue* fails to see that innocence, once lost, is unrecoverable and irreplaceable. And when we try to get it back, bad things happen, like the *Three Ds of The Gray Life* or adopting one or more of the *Three Harmful Personas*. Worse still, *Back and Blue* does not make use of one of our greatest, hardwired, and essential resources: our ability to be resilient.

"It's always darkest before the dawn," so says the English proverb first said by Thomas Fuller in 1650. And when our spirit is sick, often all the hours feel black. But as the Spanish mystic Saint John of the Cross wrote in his venerable poem, it is into the darkness that we must journey to find the light—only less widely acknowledged is that for Saint John, the darkness isn't pain, so much as an unknowable destination, and a transcendent one at that. Embarking on such a journey requires an attitude of hope, faith, or trust—take your preference—without guarantees of a "safe" passage to or assurances of finding the much-desired light.

As I mentioned, in the wake of my heart attacks, my doctors likewise could not offer me assurances or guarantees of where my heart and life would take me. The thought of entering that unknown darkness, after all the previous dark days, was honestly the last thing I wanted to do.

And then...

I remember lying in the long and whispering grass in the backyard of my home, watching a family of ducks paddle gently across a small pond at the end of the property. Across the way was a herd of black milking cows; one was scratching its back on a wire fence. The brilliant orange glow of moments before was growing dim as its source dipped behind the horizon. *One more minute*, I begged. *Please sun, just stay a little bit longer.*

An hour before I had come home from an appointment with my cardiologist. It was the much-anticipated six-month, post–heart attacks milestone check-in—one that was meant to yield decisions about my healing and overall prognosis. I had been nervous about going, not only because, once again, it felt like my life was hanging in the balance, but also because I had been lately experiencing intermittent "shadow symptoms," as I referred to them—ones that mimicked, albeit less severely, what I felt when I was having the heart attacks.

Overall, the meeting went pretty well. At the end of the exam, Dr. "Kenny," as he was affectionately known, shrugged his shoulders about the shadow symptoms and said that he wasn't particularly concerned. But he also reminded me that they (and me) were still operating in "uncharted waters," given the rarity of my condition. Then he spoke the words that have summarized my life going forward: "We've done everything we know to do for you. We don't know why this happened, and we can offer you no guarantees about life going forward because, at this point, we are in the land beyond what we can know. All the same, you must live your life. So, *go live your life.*"

Stop for a moment and consider those words: *Go live your life.*

What does that mean to you, right here, right now?

Don't read on if you're inclined. Really. Give it some thought. And as you do, notice what's happening deep inside.

Charging into Life's Unknown

In life generally, and when lost innocence strikes specifically, we often want answers to questions that simply can't be answered and assurances that can't be given. We look to our parents, teachers, experts, friends, available facts and data, scriptures, traditions, and various gods or energy forces for clear answers and trustworthy assurances. But as we mature and experience challenge and loss, we come to understand that these answers aren't always forthcoming. Indeed, perhaps they are not ever coming, or not necessarily in the time frame that would be useful for our circumstance.

When I was in graduate school studying world religion, I spent a lot of time thinking and talking about faith. But to grasp something intellectually is very different than to experience it firsthand.

As I lay in the swaying grass outside my house that evening after the appointment, overwhelmed by all the "unknowing" that lay ahead, I thought back to all those conversations in graduate school about faith. And then something in me shifted.

The setting sun across the horizon appeared as a reminder that faith is, by definition, to affirm, align with, and abide in something without knowing it absolutely. When the glow was no more and I was blanketed in dark except for a tiny sliver of moon, I not only comprehended faith's meaning but also felt a stirring along with a hopeful opening deep down—"a crack ... [where] the light gets in," in the heralded words of Leonard Cohen. As dark morphed into black and the air chilled, leaving bumps on my skin and a shiver in my lungs, and as sounds that were earlier drowned out by the day's hustle gave way to ethereal silence, I became acutely aware that, at its core, life's journey is itself about traversing darkness—but not the darkness of fear that so many people seem to resort to; rather, Saint John's darkness of faith that calls us to move forward.

Go live your life, as my doctor said in that all-important appointment suddenly meant to me, saying yes to life—co*me what may*. It was an existential trust—one that abides in unknowing, grounds in being, and surpasses all understanding. It was a living faith, as I felt it, one that beat in, under, behind, and from within the human heart—*my* heart—calling it to life; calling me to life, once more.

So, Where Do We Go Now?

Simply speaking, *Back and Blue* simply won't do. It's a bleak one-dimensional existence that can never deliver. Trust me, I know well.

In the face of lost innocence, as despairing, dislocating, and strenuous as it can be, we must not shut down and resign ourselves to what is no longer or what may never be. Instead, we must surrender ourselves to what we can't yet know or see. We must charge forward into the unknown darkness, keeping our eyes and heart open, trusting that we will find "the crack" that will bring new "light" to our life. This is faith. This is hope. This is the desire for resilience, calling to us in its unrelenting, utterly compelling, and transformational voice.

CHAPTER FOUR

THE PATH OF RESILIENCE: *LOST AND FOUND*

Only when we allow ourselves the freedom to be lost can we find the strength, courage, and fundamental resources to be found.

TOWARD JOY AND FLOURISHING

If you've made it this far, then welcome to darkness. What do you see? What do you hear? What does it feel like inside?

Seriously. Put this book down and sit with any uncertainty you're feeling for a few moments. Notice flutters, twinges, cracks, or creaks. Notice if any sadness or fear bubbles up. If so, let them surface and let them be for a minute or two. No good ever comes from denying what you feel. In fact, when adversity strikes, much of the time we lose touch with our internal and external surroundings. This disembodied sense only exacerbates the alienation or division we've already experienced.

After a few moments sitting with these feelings, dig a little deeper; open up a little wider. Shift your awareness away from any pain, fear, or sadness. And locate where inside yourself you feel good, safe, or at ease. Scan your whole body, starting at your feet and working up to your head.

Sometimes when we're in the thick of adversity, it feels as though nowhere is good, safe, or at ease. But keep going, even if you have to scan yourself a few times. It may help to envision your body as black with a small, white light floating through that space. Pause for just a moment when you feel a flicker of bright peace. As you do, think back to a time when you felt alive from having triumphed over challenge. Maybe it was something small, but meaningful; maybe the effort was herculean. Whatever it was, transport yourself to those feelings now. Sit with them for a moment and bask in their light. Now, ask yourself what is the message they're sending? What are those peaceful sensations trying to tell you? *You can . . . ? You will . . . ? You are and still can be . . . ?* This is the voice of your spirit willing you back into being.

When you're ready, return to the external world of here and now—just be sure to note what those messages said.

Unlike *Back and Blue*, Path Two, *Lost and Found*, understands that although we cannot replace our innocence, once lost, it does not have to mean the end of hope, possibility, or joy. We *can* reclaim our lives in the face of challenge or loss, and we can build a sustainable spirit that will enable us to be well every day, come what may.

While *Black and Blue* tries to undermine our happiness and make us smaller, *Lost and Found* enables our flourishing and growth. *Lost and Found* does not show us the way "back" home; rather, it reengages our resilient spirit and helps us move forward to create a new home. This home, however, may be somewhat different than the one we had before, but it can be just as *right* and *real*.

THREE MYTHS OF RESILIENCE

Come to the edge, life said.
They said, We are afraid.
Come to the edge, life said.
They came. It pushed them . . . and they flew.
GUILLAUME APOLLINAIRE

This quote has always been one of my favorites because it perfectly captures the heart and soul of resilience: the pain, the fear, being brought to the precipice of experience by forces beyond our control; to those same forces using our pain or fear as the launching point for our journey to thrive.

So often in the face of adversity, people are never able to truly "fly" because they don't understand what that means or what it requires. This is not to say they don't try. It is more that their strategies are nonstarters, and so, never get them off the ground.

Here are three big misconceptions when it comes to resilience that prevent us from "taking off."

Myth One: "Tough Guy" (Woman or Person)

The *Tough Guy* tries to be a strong, indifferent powerhouse, sucking up and swallowing pain, appearing to trudge on or breeze through adversity. Often, this is because we're trying to "save face" or we do not want to appear weak. It can also be because we're deceiving ourselves about how bad we feel, or else because we think if we don't pay attention to how we feel, then all the bad feelings will disappear. But ultimately, all these strategies break down because they fail to acknowledge that, eventually, every tank runs dry—including the energy that is ours.

The *Tough Guy* myth is a recipe for burnout. Being "strong" doesn't come from being emotionally suppressed; in fact, suppressing emotions, especially difficult ones, weakens a person. A 2013 study by the Harvard School of Public Health and the University of Rochester showed that people who bottle up their emotions have an increased chance of premature death by more than 30 percent, and their chance of getting cancer goes up by 70 percent. Studies also show that suppressing emotions can adversely affect blood pressure, memory, and self-esteem; likewise, it can lead to aggression, anxiety, and depression. Neuroscience, specifically, a study from the University of Texas, also supports what many people have long hypothesized about suppression: that the more you try to hold something back or force it down, the stronger the sensation becomes.

Resilience is not about toughing it out or "making lemonade out of lemons," as the saying goes. It doesn't mean ignoring or burying feelings of sadness, loss, or anger, nor does it mean always putting on a happy face. To the contrary. A big part of resilience is about being able to acknowledge your emotions—all of them—and allowing them to wash over you, as they come and go, monitoring their effects. And I say *all* of them because resilient people recognize the importance of emotions that make you feel *both* good and bad.

Myth Two: "No Resilience DNA"

People often think either you have resilience or you don't. For a while that's what researchers thought too. In the 1970s, when social scientists began studying resilience, their focus was on children who had experienced trauma early on. The thinking was that there was something extraordinary about kids who went on to normal development. But the findings were surprising: instead of confirming negative assumptions and deficit-focused models about children who faced adversity, they showed that resilience is actually quite ordinary—that it usually happens from our inherent adaptational systems.

To this point: Recent studies on brain functioning, genetics, and epigenetics (that is the study of how behaviors and environment can change gene activity without permanently changing the DNA sequence) have shown that resilience is an active process, not just the presence of a gene or the absence of pathology. Although individual genes and their interaction with environmental factors can both shape a person's initial responses to negative or traumatic events and influence how they think about those events, underlying brain circuits can contribute to a range of psychological strengths and behaviors, such as more adaptive ways of processing fear, experiencing positive emotions, regulating emotions, making meaning, and interacting with others.

So, while we may think, *I wasn't born that way—to be strong, to be resilient*, that's not actually the case. Resilience isn't reserved for a select few; rather, it's something that we can all participate in and master. The question is, will you?

Myth Three: "Go It Alone"

It is often assumed that to be resilient means to be "independent," that is, completely autonomous and self-contained. If we can't sort out our troubles on our own, then we must be weak, fragile, or deficient—or so it goes. But this is also a myth. As the American Psychological Association (APA) noted in its resilience report, "The primary factor in resilience is having caring and supportive relationships within and outside the family. Relationships that create love and trust, provide role models and offer encouragement and reassurance, help bolster a person's resilience."

The reason for this, it's thought, is that healthy relationships help us tamp down stress responses, even just by thinking about the relationship. In a 2011 study, spouses who felt strongly in sync with their partner felt less anticipation toward a mild electric shock; interpretation: the presence of a caring relational partner reduced feelings of anxiety or fear. Similarly, *caring touch* (i.e., gentle, tactile massage) by another person is shown to assist in trauma recovery by functioning as a tangible "anchor," and in so doing helps a person move from feeling "turned off" to becoming safe and "awake." In large-scale studies, positive relationships at one period in a person's life also predict less depression later.

And yet relationships can be with more than with just breathing individuals. Studies also show resilience is directly influenced by a person's sense of faith, hope, and love. This can come from sacred texts or scripture, prose, poetry, a beloved fable, story, or parable, even with a person from history or one that has passed on, like a friend or relative. Having something meaningful to connect with keeps our spirit strong and able to sustain during all of life's challenges.

A couple other things worth noting about resilience myths and resilience research: Although everyone has the capacity for resilience, nurture does come into play. For instance, culture can impact resilience: what is important in one culture may be less important in another. In more collectivist cultures, where the value of the group is privileged over the individual, social support and acceptance may matter more in overcoming adversity than self-efficacy, which more individualistic cultures tend toward. Research shows that resilience is influenced by the level of self-command and self-esteem a person has. The higher a person's sense of self-worth, the more likely they will be able to cope with adversity. The lower their sense of worth, the more vulnerable and helpless that person will feel, and the more likely it becomes that one problem will lead to others.

So, now that we know what resilience is not, let's look at what it is—and what it looks like in real life.

DEFINING RESILIENCE

Perhaps the best way to understand resilience is to consider those who have lived among us. Nelson Mandela is a good place to start.

Against the odds, Nelson Mandela trained and practiced as a lawyer in South Africa, helping many Black South Africans to survive the country's apartheid system. After a series of arrests for political crimes against the state, he was sentenced to life imprisonment for conspiring to overthrow the government. Mandela served twenty-seven years in prison, the majority of which were in a small cell without a bed or plumbing. He was allowed to write and receive only one letter every six months, and once a year he could meet with a visitor for half an hour. He admitted to having dark moments during these decades, but as he said, he "learned that courage [is] not the absence of fear, but the triumph over it. The brave man is not he who does not feel afraid, but he who conquers that fear," adding, "I am the captain of my soul."

Helen Keller is another obvious choice. Helen Keller's life was as normal as could be until an illness just before her second birthday left her blind and deaf. For years, she struggled with fits and tantrums, unable to communicate effectively with anyone, until Alexander Graham Bell introduced her to Anne Sullivan, whose influence would be life changing. Anne taught Helen how to read, write, and speak. Despite some individuals undermining her capabilities and intelligence, Helen went on to earn her bachelor's degree from Radcliffe College and became a fierce advocate for disability rights, woman's suffrage, and equality. "I seldom think about my limitations," Helen once said. "And they never make me sad. Perhaps there is just a touch of yearning at times; but it is vague, like a breeze among flowers . . . Character cannot be developed in ease and quiet. Only through experience of trial and suffering can the soul be strengthened, ambition inspired, and success achieved."

Of course, no list of resilient figures could be complete without Anne Frank. Anne Frank was just a girl when her family went into hiding in Nazi Germany. In the Secret Annex, the tiny, raised bunker in which she lived, Anne blossomed into a buoyant young woman in the face of death and deprivation. Imagine, being crammed with eight other people twenty-four hours a day for two years, keeping quiet and still for hours on end, listening to bombs drop all around and burglars creeping in the floors beneath, dependent on outsiders for everything you need to survive, never knowing who can be trusted not to betray you—and all this with the trials of being a teenager. Anne felt misunderstood and at odds with her family, especially her mother. She had to navigate her bourgeoning sexuality, going through crush upon crush. She had little privacy, and what she had she had to fight for. And she struggled to figure out who she was and what mattered most. Anne's struggles are known through her writing, but it was through her writing— the act of doing so—that she was able to turn hardship into an opportunity for profound self-examination that resulted in her growth and flourishing. In the midst of literal moment-to-moment existential threats, Anne blossomed into a prolific, passionate, and purposeful young woman:

I have often been downcast but never in despair; I
regard our hiding as a dangerous adventure, romantic
and interesting at the same time. In my diary, I treat all
the privations as amusing ... It's difficult in times like
these: ideals, dreams and cherished hopes rise within
us, only to be crushed by grim reality. It's a wonder I
haven't abandoned all my ideals, they seem so absurd
and impractical. Yet I cling to them because I still
believe, in spite of everything, that people are truly
good at heart.

You can almost hear her voice when the Gestapo stormed the
Secret Annex: "Think of all the beauty still left around you and be
happy."

Perhaps less known is Beethoven. Ludwig van Beethoven grew
up in an abusive, dysfunctional home, which left him rageful,
lonely, and miserable much of the time. His alcoholic father beat
him to become a prodigy like Mozart. His mother died when he
was sixteen years old. Soon after, he became the head of the house-
hold, caring for and financially supporting his two younger broth-
ers, in addition to his addled father. Music was Beethoven's only
source of refuge, self-esteem, and purpose, but eventually the situation got too much to bear, and for two years, he nearly all but
stopped composing. When the silence became also too much to
bear, he made a critical, life-changing decision: he took action to
be relieved of his cruel father's burden; and with that, new sound
burst from within him. He began to compose with a freedom and
innovation that took Austrian society by storm—that is, until his
hearing got debilitative, which sent him into a suicidal crisis. And
then, when the prospect of eternal silence seemed also too much to
face, Beethoven pivoted and made another life-changing decision:
music was, he determined, above all, a vehicle for self-expression;

rules be damned. From there he twisted, folded, minced, and sliced the established classical style. His venerated *Fifth Symphony* was a result of this effort. And yet Beethoven would have one final descension and ascension: economic hardship, a devastating love affair, and clinical deafness caused him to, again, fall into despair. But as he had done those times before, Beethoven pivoted and reinvented. In six years, this crotchety and feeble man composed a series of soul-searing and spirit-filling masterpieces that continue to inspire musicians today.

Beethoven's life, like all the lives described previously, like anyone who leverages their resilient spirit, can be summed up as both getting lost in the dark of fear and charging into the dark of faith. None of these people is a saint. They are, like any of us, simply souls struggling to find the spark of "yes" in an uncertain darkness.

These individuals also have a few things in common—*Hallmarks of Resilience*, you could say:

- ✢ Not allowing themselves to be eternally damaged, only temporarily challenged

- ✢ Remaining hopeful, open, and optimistic while also holding feelings of grief, anger, sadness, or concern

- ✢ Accepting that transition and pain are a part of life

- ✢ Remaining able to take action despite feelings of fear or lament

- ✢ Being willing to learn new things about themselves

- ✢ Relying on something meaningful for guidance or support

- ✢ Maintaining flexibility and keeping their perspective as they dealt with stress or trauma

- Remaining able to connect with other people

- Accepting and anticipating change without feeling defeated or anxious

- Maintaining the ability to take care of themselves and those who need them

- Retaining confidence in their core strengths and skills

- Finding a way to smile or laugh

When I was in graduate school, I scoured the universe of "resilience" definitions. I looked at everything from psychology to sociology, anthropology, ecology, systems theory, and the world's spiritual and religious traditions. Here are a few that jumped out.

The American Psychological Association (APA) says resilience is "the process of adapting well in the face of adversity, trauma, tragedy, threats or significant sources of stress—such as family and relationship problems, serious health problems, or workplace and financial stressors." Others have focused more on hard-won wisdom, suggesting resilience involves a conscious and positive reintegration of self that leverages lessons learned from a difficult or painful experience, or a systems approach, that being that resilience is the capacity of a dynamic system to adapt well to forces its ability to survive, function, or grow. Still others offer a more straightforward understanding, focused generally on well-being—such as the stable and healthy functioning after a highly adverse event, or that it's simply a process to harness resources to sustain well-being.

Each definition has its own particular take and can be useful in helping to understand adversity. In its clearest, most human and accessible language, and for our purposes, specifically in regard to lost innocence, I like to think of resilience as *the capacity to rally from life's trials and tribulations, strengthened by the circumstances, and better equipped to live fully, love deeply, and weather future crises with poise.*

In this way, resilience ensures that change and challenge improve, rather than hurt our lives, and fortifies rather than weakens our spirit. Resilience helps us to see that difficulties need not leave us eternally damaged, only temporarily challenged.

The key element to remember about resilience is that it's formed *because of* adversity, not *despite* it—this is a subtle difference, and not one I hear often, but, as I've experienced it, it is a critical one. "Because of" reminds us that *all* of life has something important to contribute to our lives, which should be incorporated into our story, whereas "despite" sees challenge as something that needs to be defeated, like an illness or an enemy.

CHAPTER FIVE

THE PILLARS OF RESILIENCE

So, we've looked at what resilience is and what it looks like in real life. Now let's talk about what makes resilience possible.

Drawing on multi-disciplinary research from the sciences, social sciences, humanities, and the arts, I have developed *Seven Pillars of Resilience*. And I can't tell you how often I reflect on or reference them in my own life and in my clinical work and research.

More than a general reference point, these *Seven Pillars* are like muscles that need strength-training to buttress you during moments (or durations) of adversity. The HTC framework (*Honor the Past, Transform the Present*, and *Craft a New Story for the Future*) in this book provides specific resilience "workouts."

SEVEN PILLARS OF RESILIENCE

Pillar One: Patience

Patience is a virtue—one touted in many wisdom traditions. The Judeo-Christian tradition extols patience in both the Hebrew Bible and New Testament: "A patient man is better than a warrior, and he who rules his temper, than he who takes a city," says Proverbs (16:32); in Galatians (5:21–23) patience is listed as part of the "fruit of the Spirit." In Islam, the Quran tells how Allah will "give glad tidings to those who patiently persevere." Similarly, the Sufi mystic Rumi, says, "From cane reeds, sugar. From a worm's cocoon, silk. Be patient if you can, and from sour grapes will come something sweet." For Buddhists, patience is one of the "perfections" (*paramitas*) that a bodhisattva practices to realize enlightenment. For Hindus, patience is the buoyant endurance of trying conditions and the capacity to peacefully tolerate opposites—like joy and sorrow, cold and heat, and pain and pleasure. In Taoism, Lao Tzu urges us to "wait in stillness while the mud settles." Even Friedrich Nietzsche said in his work *Human, All Too Human,* "Being able to wait is so hard that the greatest poets did not disdain to make the inability to wait the theme of their poetry."

So often patience is equated with intentional or self-imposed suffering, like we're biding our time or putting in our dues. But that attitude only feeds feelings of contempt, resentment, or indifference, which can result in the *Three Harmful Personas*: the survivor, the victim, and the martyr.

A healthy and productive way of looking at patience is learning to wander through Saint John's uncertain darkness with perspective and moderation. And when I say moderation and perspective, that doesn't mean adopting a scarcity mindset. It means conserving necessary internal resources that will keep us moving forward through that dark with even pace and our eyes wide and heart open.

So, how do we do this? Mindfulness practices can be one way.

When lost innocence strikes, our sense of time gets distorted, as we discussed. We fixate on the past; we obsess about the future; we even escape into a narrow, preoccupied present. Mindfulness helps to relocate ourselves in a safe and grounded present. Note that mindfulness is not meditation or a spiritual practice. It is an embodied, attentional state, meaning that we can feel a secure connection with our emotions and physical sensations "right now, right here." Having that secure connection goes a long way to calming feelings of fear or pain and thoughts of catastrophe or hopelessness that often bubble up while we are "wandering." In the coming chapters, mindfulness exercises are illustrated.

One of the lesser known and healthy ways to build patience is through curiosity. Think about it. When a situation is weighing on our heart or aggravating our nerves, it's hard not to fixate on it. To get relief, we often try to distract ourselves with mundane things. As we know from *The Gray Life*, a little distraction can be okay a little bit of the time, but too easily it becomes a crutch or an anesthetizer. Rather than distraction, try engagement—which is essentially what curiosity is about. Whereas distraction preoccupies our mind with trivialities, curiosity turns our attention toward something new and purposeful.

Wandering through lost innocence's unknown darkness requires a sense of grounded, embodied curiosity—"What's here? What's that—out there or else inside me? What can I learn or discover to help me moving forward?" Curiosity is more about asking questions than it is finding answers. As Albert Einstein said, "The important thing is not to stop questioning . . . never lose a holy curiosity."

Pillar Two: Meaning-Making

In Victor Frankl's venerated work *Man's Search for Meaning*, a chronicle of his experiences as a Nazi concentration camp prisoner, Frankl suggested that the primary motivation of all human beings is to discover meaning. Note, it's not the meaning of life as a whole of which he speaks; rather, meaning *in* life. "For the meaning of life differs from man to man, from day to day and from hour to hour. What matters, therefore, is not the meaning of life in general but rather the specific meaning of a person's life at a given moment."

"At a given moment" is what itself is meaningful here, for it implies that meaning can be found in all circumstances, even in the most sorrowful or painful ones. The pain of lost innocence is precisely what Frankl experienced when he arrived home after being liberated by the Allies, feeling disillusioned when there was no one to go home with—for instance, his beloved wife who died in the camps. Suffering does not end, Frankl determined, even after surviving something as horrific as genocide. His long-desired happiness didn't come from being free of physical captivity. Frankl's literal freedom still left him a "captive"—a captive in a strange place, an existential no-man's-land. The way out of it, he determined, was to create meaning.

Meaning-making is the process of how we perceive, interpret, and make sense of events in life, relationships, and ourselves. It gives us a way to organize memories and shape the narrative of an experience. Meaning also helps us reconcile incongruities in our beliefs, expectations, and attitude toward life, especially in times of adversity.

Psychologists talk about two types of meaning: *global meaning* and *situational meaning*. Global meaning refers to our general orientation to life—things such as overarching beliefs, goals, a sense of purpose, and assumptions about ourselves, others, and the world. For instance, the belief that God is benevolent or that life is fair, or that people are really good or evil at heart, or that life is random or else determined—or, as I mentioned earlier, that planes won't fall out of the sky. Situational meaning refers to how global meaning—our beliefs, goals, and assumptions—affects our reaction to a certain situation, like my brother-in-law's plane crashing into the Pacific. When our global meaning and situational meaning reinforce each other, then we have a sense of coherence, which, in turn, gives us a sense of peace. Problems erupt when these two types of meaning become incompatible: planes don't fall out of the sky—until one did, with someone I knew in it.

When it comes to lost innocence, meaning-making helps us to reconcile our sense of incoherence—or the incongruity between the beliefs that have always provided comfort or direction and the opposing reality of a situation. To make meaning from a traumatic situation, we must reconsider the experience and readjust how we understand one of the two, or both.

A mistake often made when it comes to meaning-making is thinking it is a lesson to be learned or the "moral of the story." Not so. Meaning-making is not trying to put a happy spin on pain, nor is it necessarily trying to teach us cautionary realities. Meaning-making simply helps us to broaden our thinking and feeling about a situation.

Increasingly, meaning-making has been the focus of research, especially as it concerns health and wellness. In a 2020 study, researchers at the University of California, San Diego School of Medicine, found that people who believed they had meaning in their life had better physical and mental health scores and higher cognitive function compared with those who didn't. What's more, they found that having a sense of meaning can help people stay healthy in later years. Similarly, in a 2015 study at Mount Sinai St. Luke's and Mount Sinai Roosevelt, researchers discovered that having meaning in life is associated with a 23 percent reduction in death from all causes and a 19 percent reduced risk of heart attack, stroke, or the need for coronary artery bypass surgery (CABG) or cardiac stenting.

A few final points to remember about meaning. Meaning may have a great impact on how resilient we are, but it is in the small things—ideas, gestures, connections, relationships, values, practices—where we find it. Also, meaning is not time-dependent; it is there for us when we look backward, around us, and ahead of us; the past, present, and future all have meaning waiting to be discovered. Lastly, there is a difference between demanding meaning and creating it. Demanding meaning will only result in inauthentic, short-sighted, insight; it's like vacuuming around the furniture or painting the walls around what's hung on them. Creating meaning—being curious and open, listening, questioning, reaching out, digging within—this is what keeps us moving through the dark uncertainty and what will help us find and regain the light of peace. Meaning sometimes takes some time—which is another reason why we must practice patience.

Pillar Three: Love and Connectedness

From the moment of our birth, and in many ways before, we are connected: to our biological parents through DNA; to our mother because we share and are nourished by her body for a time; to our families because they are our primary relationships throughout our lives; to society and culture that guide us collectively in how to act, how to dress, what is acceptable to say, what to believe, and what rituals to follow; to the human race through similar genetic characteristics and qualities; to the environment and our surroundings in which we live. And no matter what our effort, we stay connected in one way or another throughout the rest of our lives. Being connected is one of the realities of life; in fact, recent neuroscience research shows that we're hardwired for it: when we talk to other people, mirror neurons in our brains light up to mimic the emotions and behaviors the other person is conveying. Mathew Lieberman, director of UCLA's Social Cognitive Neuroscience lab, suggested that human beings' need for connection is even more basic than food and shelter and is the primary motivation of a person's behavior. Other neurological research shows that connection is the greatest predictor of happiness and that disconnection has a direct link to physical pain: a study at UCLA found that the part of the brain that is linked with physical distress is also stimulated when we feel socially rejected or lonely.

So, the desire to bond and belong is real. And because love—that generative "felt sense" deep inside that ties and binds us emotionally, psychologically, and spiritually to another person—is the strongest and healthiest form of human bonding and belonging, it stands to reason that love is an essential ingredient for resilience.

Love opens our hearts and lifts our spirit. It allows us to feel both vulnerable and strong. It builds trust and helps to expand our comfort zones. It makes us come alive and encourages us to make meaningful commitments. Love strengthens our confidence and builds our sense of worth. Love gives us a sense of true and enduring peace.

Brené Brown, an author and researcher known for her work on love and human connection, says that rarely can any specific response by one person make another person's hardship better, but what makes that situation bearable is love and connecting with others. Similarly, a study at the USC Marshall School of Business on the stress hormone cortisol found that sharing feelings of anxiety or stress with others significantly reduces those feelings of stress.

So often in the face of lost innocence, all we want to do is retreat from everything and everyone. Of course, taking time on our own to process whatever has happened is not only helpful, but also essential—although not as a primary strategy. It's when we become an isolated island that bad things happen—like *The Gray Life* or the *Three Harmful Personas*: the survivor, the victim, the martyr.

Reaching out and letting trusted others in is an absolute must when it comes to building a resilient spirit. And note here the word *trusted*. That also is key. Sharing struggles, difficult emotions, uncertainty, and so on can make us feel vulnerable. Now is not the time to test the waters with those who can't be counted on to be present, to listen and to hear, to have empathy and show compassion, to offer benevolent honesty and at the same time grounded hope. It's a tall order, I know, but it is what's needed when we are wandering through that dark uncertainty or unknowing. While existing friends and loved ones can help, it can also be an opportunity to reach out in new ways.

I mentioned going to cardiac rehab in the aftermath of my heart attacks. It was me, at thirty-three years old, and many people in their seventies and eighties in a windowless basement of our local hospital, walking two or three miles an hour on a treadmill, hooked up to monitors with a rainbow of wires hanging out, talking about stents, catherizations, oxygen levels, and pills with equal familiarity. And I can't forget the wonderful nurse, with a thick Boston accent, who spoke about cutting down on "sugah" and "doh-nuhs." Talk about theater of the absurd. And yet cardiac rehab was one place I felt safe—safe to talk, safe to laugh, even safe to cry when I finally got the treadmill speed up to four miles an hour and once even broke out in a jog to a chorus of cat calls and whoops and cheers. One man, Frank, in his nineties, yelled, "Honey, you're gonna break my heart all over again!"

Reaching out and letting trusted others in; loving and allowing ourselves to be loved—these are what point us, position us, protect us, and propel us through the dark uncertainty, and into that much desired spark of light.

Pillar Four: Forgiveness and Reconciling

In my trauma work with individuals who are suffering from moral injury, forgiveness and reconciling come up a great deal. In brief, moral injury is a transgression of conscience. It's what happens when a person's deeply held values, beliefs, or ways of being in the world are violated. That violation could result from things the person did themselves, things they experienced others doing, things they were forced to do against their will or better judgment, or things they couldn't stop from happening. And it's more prevalent than many would think.

Moral injury is also the epitome of lost innocence, which is one reason why it is often so difficult to heal from. For people who have transgressed their own moral compass, it's the shocking awareness that they could become, in the words of one of my clients, "the monster" they never wanted to be or ever thought they could be. For people who have been transgressed upon or betrayed, it is the dreadful awareness that others can be that monster or that the world really is home to such monsters. Moral injury, like lost innocence, makes a person question themselves, others, life, or their God. It makes them question their or others' ability to do right or be good. Moral injury deteriorates character, ideals, ambitions, and attachments. It leaves people feeling contaminated, debased, or divided in their soul knowing that something they once held dear is now sullied or destroyed.

Whether it is forgiving others or ourselves; whether it's reconciling the monster with the angel or the monster with life; whether it's a moral injury that stole our innocence or another kind of trauma or loss, forgiveness (when possible), and reconciling (which is always possible) are essential for making our way through the dark uncertainty and nurturing our resilient spirit.

Much has been written on the nature of forgiveness. One of my favorite books on the subject is *The Sunflower: On the Possibility and Limits of Forgiveness* by Simon Wiesenthal. Like Victor Frankl, Wiesenthal was a prisoner in the Nazi concentration camps, and a happenchance experience with an SS officer led him to consider his own thoughts on the subject, and then later explore a range of views on the same. It's a worthwhile read for anyone interested in going deeper into forgiveness and reconciling than we have space to do here. But as both are vital to resilience, let's look at each.

Both forgiveness and reconciling have to do with restoring ourselves when some affront or injustice has left us in pain and feeling separated. Both allow us to rebuild personal relationships, reestablish communication with those from whom we are estranged, and restore a bond of trust or faith. But whereas forgiveness is concerned with an individual relationship and a specific offense, reconciling addresses our broader sense of self in relationship to others and the world around us. Here's what I mean.

A dear friend of mine once really let me down. It was in the post–heart attacks days, and though she was the first and only friend to visit me in the hospital, some months on I noticed she wasn't very present. This was by far one of the most "trusted others" I had, so it really hurt when, at times, I needed a friend, and she wasn't seemingly available. Tragedy and adversity have a way of weeding out worthwhile relationships. But hers really mattered, and it was out of character, so I wrote her a letter and let her know how I was feeling. The next day we were at lunch at her command; "Michele, I am just so sorry; there's no excuse." There was an excuse, as I learned; she too had some difficult things going on. But the fact that she didn't use it as a crutch for her behavior, that she acknowledged not only her own actions but also my feelings, and that she owned the situation and offered a heartfelt apology with ideas of what she could do in the future to prevent this from happening again—this is why forgiving her was not only possible but also essential.

This person was, is, and will always be one of my dearest friends. But the situation also raised questions for me about friendships generally. While hers was absolutely worth the effort, including the difficult conversation that we had, I began to reconsider other relationships in my life—were they *worthwhile?* Some were to be sure; but I had to acknowledge that a few really weren't, even if that person hadn't done something specific that needed forgiving. I had given these friendships the label "trusted other" more because I had hoped they would be, or because I wanted them to be, but in reality, I knew that they could never be; they were just "other." And so, I chose to let some go.

Many people who live through hardship and loss talk about "thinning the herd," as the saying goes. Friends disappoint. People you expect to be there sometimes won't be for all manner of reasons. Human beings are imperfect and limited; this is a painful reality about life that I had to reconcile in a way I hadn't before—it was a *global meaning*—that needed to be adjusted, so that I could protect myself and set expectations about others. Only this expectation wasn't a cynical lowering the bar on friendships, meant to push others away; quite the opposite. Allowing others to be "human"—to be imperfect—helped me focus on the quality of my relationships versus the quantity, to see which ones were worthy and deserving of forgiveness when it was necessary and possible.

And yet sometimes forgiveness isn't possible.

As mentioned previously, forgiveness works at an individual level to reestablish the personal relationship between us and another. But what happens if that other has passed on, or if they refuse to apologize for their offense or refuse to hear our apology for ours? What if we desire to forgive another, but something deep inside won't allow us to? There is much research that shows the benefits of forgiveness. According to Everett L. Worthington Jr., professor of psychology at Virginia Commonwealth University, has performed life-long work on forgiveness, which shows that forgiving another lowers blood pressure, heart rate, and muscle tension; it also keeps levels of the stress hormone cortisol low and increases immunity. But other research shows that forgiving too quickly or uncritically, or what Jeffrie G. Murphy, regents' professor of law, philosophy, and religious studies at Arizona State University, calls "unqualified forgiveness," can also be harmful because it buries blame and therefore undermines legitimate self-respect and respect for the moral order.

When we're wandering through the unknown darkness brought on by lost innocence, practicing forgiveness, as we can and as is appropriate, and reconciling always, by making sure that the meaning we make out of all that's happened is coherent, is absolutely necessary. As Sue Monk Kidd said, "It's not something that happens overnight. It's an evolution of the heart"—which, again, is why patience is also so important.

Pillar Five: Self-Expression

"Insist on yourself; never imitate." The words are Ralph Waldo Emerson's from his seminal essay "Self-Reliance," but they perfectly capture the heart of self-expression.

Self-expression is often something we think of artists or children doing, or what we do when we have the confidence to stand up for ourselves. But true self-expression is the greatest example of the human spirit in action, and it's something we all must do, especially in difficult times.

And yet it is precisely in difficult times when we often have the most trouble doing so. And it's easy to understand why: the overwhelming experience of lost innocence is that our self is torn asunder or that our being is in a ball of splinters. It's no wonder that we find it hard to get up the energy to "express" ourselves.

Bessel van der Kolk, a psychiatrist and trauma expert, says that negative judgments of ourselves or others, brought on by adversity, cause our bodies and minds to tense up, which stops the flow of new information from coming in and being processed. In other words, we become "stuck." Stuckness, according to Paolo Knill, a leader in the field of expressive arts, is a state of agitated immobility that lacks choice or options or else overwhelms. It's that sense of standing on the edge of our mind, when nothing out there seems to help nor can ease our pain or, conversely, that too much is out there, which engulfs and paralyzes us.

Trauma practitioners often talk about the importance of the expressive act because it pulls us from our "stuckness" and opens us up to a new vision of existence, one that leverages all our resources and allows us to create something tangible out of hardship.

There are many ways to express ourselves—through words, movement, actions, artistic endeavors, commitments, for instance—and they can be seen in everything from our facial expressions, to our clothing, what we eat, how we speak, the space where we live, our hobbies and interests, personal ethics, spirituality, how we parent, how we care for and live with pets, where we travel or the music we listen to, how we spend our free time or manage our money, our views on politics and the environment, even how we see our legacy.

If researcher Judith Glaser is correct that advances in neuroscience show that self-expression might be one of the most important ways, if not *the* most important, for people to connect, partner, and grow together, then self-expression clearly would be beneficial no matter what your cultural orientation.

As I've considered it, self-expression, regardless of how or where it manifests, always comes down to three core issues: what we *choose*, the things we *create*, and how we *contribute*.

CHOOSE

Choice is a constant dance between our *being* (or what some call our essence) and our *actions* (or our existence). When they dance like the best of partners, in lockstep, fluid and graceful, then we know we have authentic self-expression. But what does this actually look like in real life?

We make choices at three levels: in our daily deeds; habits and patterns; and the bigger picture. Daily deeds are important when adversity strikes because even though the choices might seem small, even insignificant, they give us little bursts of feeling grounded and in command. Habits and patterns, those repeated behaviors that we develop over time, are also critical when wandering through lost innocence's uncertain darkness because we often become unaware of their influence; and if left unchecked, unhealthy habits could fester into rigidity, boredom, or obsession. Conversely, healthy habits can propel us toward new light. And choice in the bigger picture matters because it's an *attitude* toward life. Yes, we do have a choice in our attitude. Our ability to choose in any moment, in any situation, no matter how futile or frustrating, is our greatest freedom—so thought the existentialists. Said Jean-Paul Sartre, "We all must take complete responsibility for [our attitude toward] existence, because every time I act on my choices, I *will* something from nothing."

CREATE

Creation is about bringing something into being; it's not about talent, which is innate; neither is it about making something pretty or artsy. Creativity is simply about choosing to bring your imagination and intention to some situation or project. And although it may seem counterintuitive, or even impossible, to create when we're in pain, it is very much possible. Take, for example, the artist Henri Matisse, who called the latter period of his life, when he was confined to a wheelchair, his "une seconde vie," or his second life because it allowed him both to rethink what freedom really meant to him and to readjust how he expressed himself via his canvas. Author Ishmael Beah, best known for his memoir *A Long Way Gone*, used expressive writing and advocacy to give voice to his experience of being a child soldier in Sierra Leone and his eventual escape and difficult transition to a new life in the United States. Similarly, the African American scientist and inventor George Washington Carver, after being rejected by universities, used his homesteading interest to eventually get a graduate degree in Botany and improve the agricultural economy of the United States. Each of these people, like countless others throughout time and across culture, discovered a new vision or voice in the dark uncertainty—one that not only served as balm for pain but also helped them transform their trauma into healing.

There is another aspect to creating that isn't often talked about: creative destruction. Although all creations are sacred, sometimes our best ones emerge out of the demise of other creations. I'm reminded of the mythical phoenix. The phoenix is an ancient symbol for invincibility, creativity, hope, and rebirth. When the sacred bird reaches the end of its life, it is said to set itself ablaze in a self-made nest, only then to rise from the ashes whole and begin its life anew. When faced with lost innocence, sometimes we have to say goodbye to some part of ourselves, to something we've created, to grow. Creative destruction is, in essence, both an end and a beginning.

Of course, the choice to create is itself an act of creation. Therefore, it's less important to focus on what we create, but rather that we do.

CONTRIBUTE

"We have to go into the despair and go beyond it, by working and doing for someone else, by using it for something else." These are the words of Elie Wiesel, the Nobel Laureate, esteemed professor, and author of the acclaimed book *Night*, which, like Frankl's and Wiesenthal's, chronicles his experience in the Nazi concentration camps during World War II. They also sum up what more and more scientific research shows: that finding purpose in darkness, one that specifically gives support to others, has a significant impact on our ability to be resilient.

For instance, some researchers talk about the "helper's high," that euphoric feeling people experience after doing a good deed or an act of kindness. In a study at the National Institutes of Health, individuals who contributed their time by volunteering or donating money were 42 percent more likely to be happy than those who didn't. The study likewise found that those activities activated the same areas of the brain that are stimulated by the pleasures of food and sex.

Studies also show that helping others buttresses our body from the damaging effects of stress. For instance, people who volunteered their time also had lower levels of the stress hormone cortisol on the days they worked. Similarly, a study in Detroit found that challenging life events more negatively affected people who were less helpful to others, whereas those who did help appeared to erase the damaging physical effects of stressful experiences.

Contributing is also about offering our *self*, not just our time or money. Emily A. Greenfield, an associate professor of social work at Rutgers University, speaks about "felt obligation," that is, people who would sacrifice something of their own if it would help another person. Her research shows that, indeed, those individuals who had higher levels of felt obligation were better equipped to cope with their own adversities, the theory being that caring for others helps us regulate our emotions and gain a sense of control.

Evolution has wired us to support one another through kindness, generosity, goodwill, and benevolent giving because supporting one another has also proven to be instrumental in human survival. Many wisdom traditions call this support *grace*: from the

Latin *gratia*, or what has been kindly done for you. Contribution not only benefits others; when we're motivated by a generosity of spirit, we too benefit. Said Jesuit priest Anthony de Mello, "Charity is really self-interest masquerading under the form of altruism . . . I give myself the pleasure of pleasing others"; the Dalai Lama refers to it as "selfish altruism."

Self-expression is the act of bringing something deep within us into observable form. When faced with adversity, it's not merely making something out of nothing; it is making something out of pain, which is nothing short of transformative. So, when trying to build a resilient spirit, while ambling through the uncertain darkness, reach in, dig down, and harness your unique inner voice and vision, and "express."

Pillar Six: Self-Mastery

We never want to seize control more than when we don't have it.

I remember one day a few weeks post–heart attacks standing in my bedroom closet, reaching for a sweater when the phone rang. It was the middle of July in steamy, sweltering New England, and while everyone else was in tank tops and shorts, I had goose bumps under many layers. In addition to the triple blood-thinning regimen that turned my blood into the consistency of water, which left me using nothing sharper than a butter knife, I was also on various blood pressure medications that left me fainting left and right and unable to drive a car for some time.

When I quickly turned to answer the phone, everything in my periphery also began to rotate—and then the light dimmed and everything went dark. I awoke on the rug on my back, with a small, wet, sandpaper tongue having its way with my forehead. I managed to pull myself up to a sitting position, still groggy. As the room came into view, I realized I was sitting in a heap of knit; apparently the shelf that held my sweaters had toppled with me.

Without thinking, I pushed onto my knees and tried to stand—with the same success as a toddler trying to take her first step. Boom! I plummeted again. Three more times I pushed up and tumbled down. Finally, I was up but teetering.

My indignance at my precarious state, combined with an instinct to make the closet shelf submit, commandeered my good sense. When I bent over to pick up the shelf and heaved it up over my head, swaying as I did, a strange sensation rippled through my upper body. And then my cardiologist's voice yelled out, "Lift nothing over ten pounds or above your shoulders." Down fell the shelf, scaring the poor cat. Down fell me, again, in an equal state of fear. *I've done it*, I thought. *Another heart attack—this one worse. I've killed myself!* I sat there on the floor watching the life I had just gotten back flash in front of my eyes again. And then rage engulfed me, like a thirteen-alarm fire. All I remember is picking up a shoe on the floor next to me and whipping against the floor again and again and again. *Stupid! This whole thing is just so stupid! How can I ever do anything again?!*

And then my cardiac-geneticist's voice filled my ears, "You should not do any strenuous activities, especially any sudden or jarring movements." *Well, that's it*, I determined, looking at the abandoned shoe and bursting into tears. *The nail in my coffin. I'm just going to wait here to die.*

Research suggests the need for control—in life, in our environment—is a biological imperative for survival. Actually, it's the *perception* of control that we find rewarding because it buffers our stress and allows us to act with intention and determination. But here's the thing, one of those tough truths we'd rather not hear but would do well to acknowledge: we can't always control what happens—no matter how hard we work, believe, study, or pray. Life simply doesn't work that way.

Self-mastery is often thought to be self-control—or, more specifically, the ability to restrain the fearful and unruly parts of ourselves. Although emotions do factor into it, self-mastery is not about subjugating these parts; in fact, it's not at all about subjugation or even control.

Self-mastery is the present-focused realization that we can always be in command of ourselves—body, mind, and spirit—even while accepting that we may not be able to control all situations or outcomes. It's about learning how to *struggle well* by being mindful of our feelings, thoughts, and deeds, so that in any moment, no matter how difficult, we can make an intentional *choice* (there's that word again) to follow our own good sense and moral compass.

Victor Frankl said that there is a space between stimulus and response and that our ability to heal and grow lies in that space—in our *response* to that space. So, what does is take, when we're standing in that liminal uncertain darkness to find the power to *choose* a healthy response? It takes turning inward.

Unlike self-expression, which is concerned with bringing the inner out, self-mastery is about diving deep into our inner landscape. It's not a place that most of us are used to going; as we mature out of childhood and into adults, we learn to prioritize the world around us, often only paying attention to our bodies when some need requires satisfying; for instance, when we're hungry, thirsty, or aroused, or when we are in pain or exhausted. And yet there's a whole world of emotions, feelings, and sensations beneath the surface that is inundating us with messages at every moment.

Research at the University of Toronto suggests that there are different ways of paying attention: exteroception, which focuses on what's going on around us, and interoception, which traverses what's going on within—signals about how our body is feeling inside, like a growling stomach, dry mouth, racing heart, heavy breathing, or tense muscles. All of these and other sensations have much to say about how we feel, what we think, and how we act in each moment.

In ordinary life, with all the external distractions, it's easy to lose sight of what's going on inside, but as trauma research shows, adversity can make us become quite disembodied. Said Bessel van der Kolk, "The only way we can change the way we feel is by becoming aware of our inner experience and learning to befriend what is going on inside ourselves."

In the midst of lost innocence, turning our attention inward can be distressing because we come face to face with emotions that are uncomfortable. But distracting, denying, or distorting them, as we learned with *The Gray Life*, won't make them go away. The adage, "what we resist persists," or what Dan Wagner at Harvard University calls an "ironic process," really is true.

Like charging into the uncertain darkness with faith, we too need to charge into the cavern within. There, we don't try to quash unpleasant emotions or judge them as wrong or weak. We give them space and time to tell us something new about what's going on. We observe and get curious (there's that word again) about what basic need or fundamental desire is not getting met. All of this allows us to regain a sense of calm and perspective that leaves us not stupidly hoisting a heavy shelf over our head when it could endanger us or whipping a shoe against a wall because life feels out of control.

Mindfulness practices, which we'll discuss in the following chapters, are one way to explore this internal space; they help us to stay alert and be focused without becoming rigid or narrow. One of the challenges of entering this space is getting prepared. Grounding practices (or "earthing" as it is sometimes called), which we'll also discuss, can help to do that.

Like other *Pillars of Resilience*, self-mastery requires patience, courage, and active engagement. It's not always easy to befriend and give voice to our pain; it's not always possible to control all outcomes. But it is possible for us to be in command of ourselves—to struggle well during adversity. And it is absolutely necessary for building a resilient spirit.

Pillar Seven: Dynamic Balance

"Waves come in sets of seven." This was the first piece of advice my father gave me when I was a little girl. And I can't tell you how many times that advice has come in handy, especially one particular day.

It was late afternoon, three, maybe four o'clock. The wind had picked up from the north and was blowing the sea into a sizeable chop. My family and I had been sprawled out at Wasque Beach on Martha's Vineyard since early that morning. As usual, I was playing in the water, on tippy-toes, bouncing up and down, weightless and uninhibited, waiting as the waves grew taller and taller. In the distance, one wave was building—the curve in the middle getting more pronounced. Did I wait too long or dive too soon? I have no idea. All I remember is feeling a crash over my head; flow pulling me down; spinning round and round, like clothes in a washer; water rushing, choking, blocking every orifice. My eyes forced open, and I tried to reorient, but everywhere I looked all I could see was muddy green. The sonorous drone flooding my ears was deafening. And my head collided with a wall of sand. Then my arms started to flail like a newly caged bird. And my body tightened as if it had rigor mortis. And then I was sinking, fast—in what direction I didn't know.

And that was the moment I first felt death—that nanosecond of blackness, absolute nothingness. And then I heard his voice—like the divine with a Philly accent: "Swim toward the light."

My father is from Philadelphia, and while we joke that he's my "Not-so-Zen Dad," given his lack of explicit spirituality, his words about how to save myself in the surf have deeply resonated because they apply so profoundly to the challenges we face when life unexpectedly throws us into chaos. Said my dad of the sea, "Mother Nature *always* wins. There are lots of things you'll need to fight for and against in life, but she isn't one of them. You'll lose every time. But you can't give up either because you also don't want to drown. So, the first thing you do when you're overwhelmed and scared is to relax. Tense muscles are paralyzing . . . they'll turn you into lead. You need to stay buoyant. If you relax, it'll also focus you and get you thinking straight again—which *will* help."

And "It's gonna be dark down in the water, and even though you won't want to, you have to keep your eyes open and see what's going on. It may hurt, and you may not like what you see . . . hell, you may not actually see anything specific because it's too murky; but trust me, if you look around, you *will* see the light . . . and that's where you want to be. So, once you find it, swim like hell toward it. And I promise, if you do, you'll get to the surface safely and be able to breathe again."

He also said, "Don't think you're out of the woods yet. You still have to get to shore . . . and your body's going to be exhausted. Now, if there's a strong rip (i.e., current), here is where you use Mother Nature to your benefit. You have to let the current be your guide . . . Not like some piece of driftwood. You need to steer yourself while in that flow. Stay alert. Focus on the shoreline and getting to it. But remember, it's not a race. Don't waste all your energy fighting to get there. Just stay relaxed . . . move with the pull of water, all the while edging toward the shore. And listen, it doesn't matter how far down the beach you eventually end up. You can always walk back to where you started. The point is just to get there."

And, finally, he said, "The last thing to know is this: waves come in sets of seven. That means while the journey back to solid ground may still be rough, you will also have some lulls. You gotta ride the 'rough' and lay back in the 'lull.' And keep reminding yourself that fighting against the forces will only suck out everything you have. Remember, you can't change Mother Nature. You have to make her your friend."

This story perfectly captures the spirit of *Dynamic Balance*: in the midst of uncertain darkness, we must become a tree in the wind, bending to its might, or a boat in the current, "faring on the water's flowing flood," as the Ancient Egyptians tell us—adjusting with poise and confidence through changing situations.

I call this "faring" *Dynamic Balance* because balance alone is a myth; nothing in life can remain completely at rest except that which is lifeless, dead. When faced with adversity, stasis—that is *not* moving with the forces—will be the death of your spirit.

Moving with the forces does not mean saying apathetically or with resignation, "Ya, fine, whatever happens . . ." It means finding stability amid chaos or change by saying, "I'm okay, come what may." Dynamic balance goes back to that notion of surrender: we don't always know what or when; we can't always know how or why; we don't know what the future holds, and not even the experts can always provide the answers we crave. Yet we must live and live well.

Practicing the *Seven Pillars of Resilience* may not come immediately or easily. Of all the pillars, *Dynamic Balance* can feel at times the most strenuous because it gets to the heart of the human condition: seasons always change and "all things must pass." In life, we will enter the unknown darkness, with no guarantees about the outcome. Perhaps we enter this unknown at birth; perhaps it is exacerbated when adversity strikes. And while we try to deny it until circumstances no longer permit, it always nags at the back of our minds and feeds all the little fears that undermine us and pull us toward living a "gray," inauthentic life. But as Albert Camus observed when mired in his own dark, cold winter, "I found in me an invincible summer."

Invincibility breeds stability—invincibility defined as that kernel of calm deep within our being brought on by befriending

Mother Nature (or life's undeniable forces); "relaxing" into the situation, so that we stay supple, not rigid; "riding the waves" of emotion and "focusing" on where we want to go; and "keeping our eyes open" to the reality of the situation, even though it's hard or it hurts; always actively "swimming toward the light," because meaning, connection, beauty, and peace *still* can be ours. This is what dynamic balance is all about and it is key to building a resilient spirit.

CHAPTER SIX

NAVIGATING THE
PATH OF RESILIENCE

"No man ever steps in the same river twice," said the Greek philosopher Heraclitus. "You can't go home again," wrote the author Thomas Wolfe. *Lost and Found* is the *Path of Resilience* because it understands that things morph, places change, that everything in life is in a constant state of transformation. Sometimes this means that the way we live, who we live with or love, the things we believe in or expect to be there shift or else are taken away. Sometimes life's events force us to leave "home"; other times "home" leaves us.

I once heard it said that home exists only in the maps of our memory. But that is a *Back and Blue* way to think about home. Home is not a place, a person, or a thing by itself, as meaningful as each one may be. "Home" is a felt sense within us that people, places, and things all help to engender. To be sure, no one of these can be replicated, but our sense of home can be re-created.

Lost and Found doesn't ask us to deny, minimize, or indulge our lost innocence or that lost feeling of "home," but neither does it encourage us to clone how it was. Rather, it asks us to reconsider what it can be; and "what it can be" is just as *right* and *real*. But doing this takes some help from our spirit.

REALIZING AND ENGAGING OUR SPIRIT

As I said earlier, like an idea, an opinion, a personality, or a dream, everyone has spirit. But as busy, modern people, spirit can sometimes be hard to get our heads around, which makes it difficult to leverage when we're faced with the challenge of lost innocence.

For centuries people have puzzled over and sometimes fought about spirit—and it's a shame because that means they've lost the essence of spirit. Here's a great metaphor for spirit: spirit is the rhythmic beating, the pumping heart, the flowing stream, the moving particles, the streaming video, the hot circuit, the encoding system that keeps us both going and growing.

Simply speaking, spirit is the animating energy at the core of our lives that directs us toward who we really are and what we most *desire* to do. Now, I use the word *desire* here very purposely. The desire I'm talking about is not the one often associated with craving or lust; it is the purer, original form dating back millennia—from the Latin *desiderare*, meaning "long for, wish for"; from the phrase *"de sidere"* or "await what the stars will bring."

THE POWER OF DESIRE TO MOTIVATE OUR SPIRIT

For a long time, and in large part, our understanding of human motivation, wellness, and flourishing has been based on Abraham Maslow's Hierarchy of Needs. In short, Maslow suggested that our basic needs, including safety, security, and sustenance, must be met before we can meet our "higher" psychological and social needs, such as personal esteem, intimacy, friendship, and, the pinnacle, realizing our individual potential, or achieving, as he termed it, "self-actualization" or "self-transcendence." The problem with this is that it overlooks an important distinction about human motivation and fails to understand the crucial role of spirit in human life—especially in difficult times.

To say that inner awareness, personal drive, personal development, and spiritual enlightenment depend on first meeting one's "lower" or basic needs ignores centuries of examples to the contrary. By this standard, Moses, Jesus, Mohammad, the Buddha, or any other of history's gurus, masters, sages, or geniuses who found themselves wanting of ready sustenance, sex, security, society, and self-esteem could never have achieved the self-actualization that scholars and practitioners alike agree they did.

And yet this same dynamic is also evidenced outside such exalted figures. Over and over, we have witnessed citizens of some of the world's most impoverished, conflicted, and vulnerable communities making meaning where there is pain. Countless times we have observed destitute individuals standing strong, confident, and purposeful, sometimes literally singing their joy as they are pulled from disaster, barely breathing and despite the ruin of their lives. We have even seen how shared scarcity or despair can not only bring people together, garnering newfound respect for and admiration of the "other," but also evoke a sense of integrity, humility, reverence, and resourcefulness. Consider the devastation in East Asia when the tsunami struck in the early aughts, or Hurricanes Katrina, Harvey, and Maria in the United States and Puerto Rico, or Haiti in the aftermath of the 2010 earthquake, or the cave-in in Chile, which trapped thirty-three miners. It can also be illustrated by the beautifully haunting narratives and music that came from the horrors of the Irish famine or the celebratory ritual communal praise dances of destitute Africans and Native Americans, or in the African American spirituals that grew out of the slave experience, or in the expressions of resilience found in the art and culture produced by prisoners in Nazi death camps.

To be sure, one need not be affluent to gain respect from others or to experience awe and wonder. Neither does a person need to be employed to spark their imagination or fulfill their potential. Indeed, it is not the presence of "lower" needs that typically stir a person's spirit to creativity, spontaneity, resourcefulness, and problem-solving; nor does it necessarily motivate them to seek a deeper understanding of life or a more actuated sense of self. Often it is the absence of or challenge to these very things that does.

Maslow's hierarchy doesn't take into account the nuisances of the human condition, positive emotions in times of adversity, and the fundamental resilience of the human spirit. As I've considered it, perhaps a better way to think about human motivation and flourishing is to distinguish between three interrelated components: *needs*, which secure our lives; *wants*, which enhance our lives; and *desires*, which define our lives. Here's what I mean.

Needs are what our bodies require to survive, for instance, food, water, oxygen, safety, and security. We depend on them, quite literally, for our survival. Wants are what our minds tell us we'd like to have to enhance our lives, such as social validation, money and status, a particular skill set, or else something that gives us personal pleasure, such as luxury purchases, sumptuous meals, and surplus leisure time. A healthy want comes from a healthy ego; the same way a healthy ego mediates between craving and conscience, a healthy want finds the sweet spot between excess and scarcity. When the equilibrium is lost, and wants are left unfulfilled, bad things happen. The best way to avoid losing this equilibrium is to align our wants with a desire. So, what's a desire?

Desires are what we inherently and essentially long for to be happy and well. They are more fulfilling than mere survival needs, but also more enduring and rooted than wants. Desires are energized and empowered by the potential for true joy, contentment, self-worth, and peace. They are our core; they directly motivate our spirit; and they sustain us in all circumstances throughout our lives.

INTRODUCING THE *SIX FUNDAMENTAL HUMAN DESIRES*

When I was in graduate school studying world religion, I became intrigued by what, if anything, undergirds all the wisdom and spiritual traditions. I had no interest in diluting or melting them into one. I was more curious about what was beneath and beyond belief. After much research, I arrived at what I termed the *Six Fundamental Human Desires*:

Meaning

Meaning helps us to *make sense of life* and *find significance in life*. It satisfies our desire to have a life filled with understanding and awareness, peace and satisfaction. Meaning helps us to see how we fit into the world and that greatly shapes the stories we live by. Meaning gives us the sense that we, others, and certain things in life matter, and so helps us to craft a rich and rewarding existence.

Meaning gives us faith that within each moment or each situation in which we find ourselves, there is some *kernel of truth*—something important and worthwhile that can orient us, carry us forward, and help us to be well.

Purpose

Purpose grounds and motivates us, unifies our life, and directs us toward some *ultimate concern* or "North Star" around which we shape our lives. Purpose satisfies our desire to have a reason to get up in the morning and go to bed at night feeling as though we've done something important or worthwhile. Purpose gives us faith that we have "miles to go before we sleep."

Value

Value helps us determine what we give *priority* and *precedence* to, and what we *pursue* in life. Values satisfy our desire to have something to work for, find deserving, invest in, and live by. Values give us faith that there are certain things we can always turn to and rely on to keep our integrity intact and us headed in the right direction.

Connection

Connection helps us *relate to* and *form relationships with* others and the world around us. Connection satisfies our desire to bond and belong—to have a type of familial warmth and security. Connection gives us faith in the very real power of trust, intimacy, community, empathy, and love.

Resilience

Resilience shows us how to flourish, not despite but *because of* adversity, in a way that improves rather than hurts our lives and fortifies rather than weakens our spirit. Resilience satisfies our desire to live fully, love deeply, and thrive every day, come what may. Resilience gives us faith that life is always worth living.

Transcendence

Transcendence *wakes us up to the fullness of life*—to experience something greater than our daily tasks and to-do lists, something truly sublime or divine. Transcendence satisfies our desire for wonder and awe. Transcendence gives us faith that there are things in life that will always inspire, encourage, humble, and excite us.

Each of us experiences, satisfies, and expresses these six desires uniquely, giving life its infinite variety. But taken together, they are what all the great traditions, whether spiritual or secular, each in their own way, using their own language, care about and try to make real for people's lives. They are the glue that holds humanity together. They reach beneath and beyond background and belief. And they are the key to building a sustainable spirit in the face of life's challenges.

NAVIGATING THE PATH
OF *LOST AND FOUND*

"I went to the woods because I wished to live deliberately, to front only the essential facts of life, and see if I could not learn what it had to teach, and not, when I came to die, discover that I had not lived." These are the words of the transcendentalist Henry David Thoreau in his seminal book *Walden.* It's part memoir, part satire, and part spiritual quest, and it details his experiences living alone in a small cabin in the woods near Concord, Massachusetts.

I grew up in Massachusetts and lived near those woods for a time; one day I wandered into them when I was feeling rather lost. It was late November, around three in the afternoon, nearly six months post–heart attacks. The sky was gray and indifferent, like the squirrel perched motionless on a sagging tree. Not even the snow could decide whether to cover the ground. The only conviction seemed to be the cold, and it was pretty decided: thirty-four degrees read the digital thermostat in my car when I ventured outside, although for me and my thin blood it felt like minus fifteen.

Months before, as I mentioned, I had charged into the dark uncertainty with faith, and although there had been some small successes—such as lowering my slew of medication, so at least I could drive, and graduating from cardiac rehab, so at least I could feel confident that I could move safely and with some verve—I had also lately hit a wall. I still felt very displaced and disjointed. I kept thinking, *I'm a thirty-three-year-old woman who had two heart attacks, three stents, and a pill case the size of Methuselah's, when most of my similarly aged friends were having kids, running marathons, and preparing to go skiing and have a long life.* When I looked in the mirror all I could see was young, but what I felt like inside was very, very old. It wasn't just that I tired easily and still moved somewhat like a turtle. It was also an emotional, existential weariness. As the acute danger phase had seemingly passed, and the new rhythm of life-with-SCAD began to settle in, so too did the awareness that my life really *had* changed in meaningful ways and that it would continue to change in ways I couldn't predict, assuming it continued, with the ebb and flow of time.

And there was the kicker: time. It felt completely topsy-turvy. I knew I couldn't go back to the innocent "good old days," when I had a pure, undamaged heart. The future was still up in the air, given the precariousness of my condition. Lots of people advised me to "live in the now," but as much as I've always loved stopping to smell life's flowers, I also loved to dream with purpose—but that brought me back to the issue of whether I had a future or for how long. Honestly, for a while, it felt as though I was stumbling through, rather than charging into, the dark.

On that dreary day, I stood at the edge of Walden Pond, my boot tips tapping intermittently at the surrounding layer of ice, searching the sky as it turned from steel to charcoal, running over in my mind my new "essential facts of life," hoping the surrounding wilderness would stir some moment of inspiration. Nothing came.

I headed back through the woods trying to figure out a path back. I must not have been paying attention when I wandered in and, at that moment, I wasn't sure how to get out. The rush of fear can produce a rush of warmth thanks to pumping adrenaline. As I much as I hate to be scared, right then I rather wished I was; every one of my limbs and extremities was losing feeling, and the day was losing light. While I took comfort that I had a charged cell phone with reception, I was really annoyed at myself for not "keeping my eyes open" to my surroundings, as the "divine with a Philly accent" (aka Dad) had once told me.

"When we are lost in the woods, the sight of a signpost is a great matter," said C. S. Lewis. *No kidding*, I thought, surveying the area with a loud sigh. After a few fits and starts, finally, I spotted a wooden board nailed to a tree in the shape of an arrow: "Parking, this way."

Even those of us with a good sense of direction benefit from a sign or GPS, so that we can better navigate our trip's terrain or else know what to expect throughout each stage of the journey.

As discussed, the experience of lost innocence can be somewhat (or very much) traumatic, and often this causes changes in how we see ourselves, others, and the world around us, especially how we locate them in time. When we travel down the path of *Lost and Found*, we require a special positioning system, one that leverages our spirit and locates us in the fullness of time, so that we can regain a sense of wholeness—or what I like to think of as an embodied sense of coherence.

THE IMPORTANCE OF COHERENCE

Aaron Antonovsky, a medical sociologist, developed the concept of sense of coherence (SOC), based on the idea that our normal human state is chaos and challenge, rather than stability. He wanted to know why some people maintain a positive attitude and good health when faced with hardship or stress, while others do not.

Antonovsky defined a sense of coherence as an overarching orientation that expresses the extent to which we can confidently comprehend life in some rational way; confidently manage life in a way that leverages our strengths and available resources; and confidently endure life's difficult situations because we recognize that our lives have relevance, significance, and value.

The sense of coherence Antonovsky described underscores some of the *Seven Pillars of Resilience*, including meaning-making, self-expression, and dynamic balance. His research found that people who had a higher sense of coherence showed a greater ability to handle adversity and better health. At first Antonovsky thought that a sense of coherence was relatively stable over time, but further research showed that it is mutable: a person's sense of coherence can develop over their life cycle and may increase with age. If it's true that a sense of coherence is not a fixed state and that it is based in our own perceptions, then so too can it intentionally and positively shift with time.

Speaking of time . . .

COHERENCE AND PERSPECTIVE

Where do you live? The past? The present? The future? Or some combination thereof? More to the point, *how* do you live there?

Stanford University psychology professor emeritus Philip Zimbardo suggested we are all time travelers, bouncing back and forth between what was, what is, and what will be; he also suggested that how easily we move between them is pivotal in our ability to be well and get through difficult times.

Zimbardo proposed the idea of *time perspective*, meaning that our perception of time influences our emotions, judgments, decisions, and actions. It goes that we all inhabit multiple time zones, formed in childhood, and shaped by education, culture, economics, and social class. By the time we have become adults, most of us will have developed a preferred orientation for one time frame over others. Like Antonovsky's sense of coherence, Zimbardo believes that our time perspective is not fixed—that we can learn to shift our attention between the past, present, and future depending on a given situation.

While both approaches on their own have merit and have proven to be beneficial for individuals' health and well-being, I want to propose a third approach that leverages and builds off each, but is specifically designed for working through adversity, trauma, and lost innocence. I call it a *coherent sense of time*, and it is the special positioning system I mentioned when we travel down the path of *Lost and Found*.

NURTURING A COHERENT SENSE OF TIME

When something is coherent, there is the sense that various individual parts have become united as an integrated whole. In the case of the trauma of lost innocence, that whole is time, which can easily become fragmented. We fixate on the past, reliving what we had and have lost, or as David Eagleman, a neuroscientist at Baylor College of Medicine, describes it, we "lock [our] eyes onto painful events in the rear-view mirror." We live in a world of regrets and what could have been, ignoring "the now" and forgoing the future. Other times we block out the past and avoid the future by escaping into the present. We may tell ourselves we're taking one day at a time, but then we realize that the mail is still unopened, and the bills are piling up; or that we've put off making important decisions or are evading responsibilities; or that we're indulging our hedonic tendencies a little (or a lot) too much—such as spending, drinking, sex, and other risky or addictive behaviors; or that we're focusing so much on our own ego-wants that we're ignoring the essential needs and desires of important others; that we've turned the much-touted motto "be here now" into "me here now." Of course, the future can also become a place to run to; if the past is too painful and the present too hopeless or dangerous, then the future gives us something constructive to work toward—only with all the constant toiling, planning, worrying, and attempts to control it, our restlessness about what we lost never gets reconciled, and we miss out on the small joys of the here and now.

Time is something we often take for granted, never realizing how much our perspective can affect how we feel, think, and act. When we're wandering in lost innocence's dark uncertainty, it's even easier to overlook. Having an incoherent sense of time means that we're stuck in one frame—or even two frames; but we are definitely not living in all frames, and so are left disjointed.

When we have a coherent sense of time, we can see our-selves *fully* in the past, present, and future. That means holding each time frame with equal value and importance and viewing each one with *grounded hope* and *benevolent honesty*.

"Grounded hope" is a phrase coined by David B. Feldman and Lee Daniel Kravetz to describe what many in the field of resilience and posttraumatic growth have come to believe: that "happy think" alone isn't the way out of adversity. In other words, in the face of challenge or loss, optimism about oneself or life can be a good thing, so long as it's based in reality; only then can we make the appropriate choices that give form to how we respond.

"Benevolent honesty" is a phrase I coined to describe a sim-ilar kind of clear-eyed, no-rose-colored glasses, no blinders, no exaggeration way to engage with challenge or loss, but the key here is to do so with kindness and compassion—a gentleness with ourselves and others as we absorb new realities.

Developing a coherent sense of time requires us to step into each frame and reengage and integrate our experiences, so that we can *Honor the Past, Transform the Present,* and *Craft a New Story for the Future.*

These are the three markers along the path of *Lost and Found* that will see us safely and confidently through lost innocence's dark uncertainty and into new light.

PART 2

Honor the Past,
Transform the Present,
Craft a New Story for
the Future

INTRODUCING "HTC"

"HTC," if you haven't guessed, is the acronym I use to talk about the tripartite model for resilience: H = *Honor the Past*; T = *Transform the Present*; and C = *Craft a New Story for the Future*. In the following sections, we will go deep into each—we'll discuss the goal or purpose for that frame; the challenge in meeting it, or rather, what it will take to achieve that goal; and then a plan of action, including exercises, practices, and inspirations, for doing it successfully, as well as ways to commit to sustaining it.

I've heard it said that a seed fears neither light nor darkness; rather, it uses both to grow. It's a great metaphor for HTC. *Honor the Past* is about finding seeds of hope, or "kernels of truth," as I like to think of them, in our pain. It's heart-centered work with meaning-making, forgiveness and reconciling, and patience at its core. Because it's not always easy to "touch the murky places," as trauma expert Eugene T. Gendlin describes it, "slow and steady" will be our motto. You'll learn how to drop in and out of your painful experience, so that it keeps you safely engaged and open to insight without being overwhelmed or dysregulated. In *Transform the Present*, we'll plant and nurture those seeds by learning how to say yes to life again. Meaning-making and patience will still be important, but here love and connection, self-expression, self-mastery, and dynamic balance come to the fore. *Craft a New Story for the Future* allows us to reap the seed-turned-fruit by putting into action what specifically we're saying yes to—it's an intentional reshaping and retelling of the story that our life *now desires* to tell.

So, let's discover how to *Honor the Past*.

CHAPTER SEVEN

STEP 1

HONOR THE PAST

Sometimes the miracle is not in the restoration of what was, but in the courage to reconcile yourself to what is and flourish because of it.

It seems cliché to say that what doesn't kill us makes us stronger; moreover, that our specific experience of pain or loss is actually a good thing. Tell this to the man who loses his job and has a spouse and three kids to feed. Tell this to the parents who lose a child to violence, drugs, or suicide. Tell this to the woman who finds a lump and wonders if she will be around to see her kids grow up. And tell this to the adolescent who is abused by a trusted friend or relation. There is simply no getting around the fact that meaningful loss, especially the loss of innocence, is absolute, irreducible, and irreplaceable. And no simple cliché, however well intended, can will it away.

So, why then do we need to *Honor the Past?* Won't this only increase our pain? Shouldn't we just "put the past behind us" and soldier on? The short answer is no and no.

Muscling the past into some old memory trunk and burying it deep within an internal emotional graveyard is nothing more than selective amnesia—an unproductive and unsustainable escapist strategy that forces us to cut off from important aspects of who we are and from events or people who have shaped our lives to this point. It's a recipe for *The Gray Life*—an incoherent life of distraction, denial, and distortion—and, as we know, this is no life at all. What we resist, persists—as we also know.

And yet wallowing in the past, or constantly reliving past traumas or adverse experiences, is also unhealthy; in fact, it can be extremely destructive. Research shows that even thinking about unresolved conflict in certain ways can cause torrents of stress chemicals to surge throughout our body to measurably harmful ends, or just recalling an experience that triggers anger, resentment, or disgust increases heart rate and blood pressure. Research also shows that people who are chronically anxious or angry are at greater risk for heart attacks and other cardiovascular disease, as well as weakened immune systems. Fixating on the past is like getting swallowed up in a sinkhole of negativity and fatalism, from which it is very difficult to climb out.

Like Goldilocks who eventually found "just the right amount," the key to engaging the past lies in fitting it with the right lens. In *Honor the Past*, it's not that we're saying the events that precipitated our pain and caused our lost innocence are unimportant or even just. Rather, we are affirming that *every* aspect of life—good, bad, happy, sad, joyful, or painful—has a key role to play in making us who we are today and who we will be tomorrow. Moreover, that in every experience throughout our lives, including distressing ones, there is a *kernel of sacred truth*—a message or meaning, an insight that is inherently worthy and honorable to carry with us and even inspire us going forward; that in pain there are always seeds of hope to plant.

The challenge of and opportunity in *Honor the Past* lies not in subjugating or forgetting pain, nor condoning wrongs or minimizing hurt, but rather in finding that sacred truth and nourishing those seeds of hope as a source for growth and empowerment.

Honor the Past is a transformative experience for a few simple yet profound reasons:

1. Because it shows us how to reconcile what was and what is, or may never be, in a way that opens us up to peace. That peace may be within us, in our relationships, or in life generally.

2. Because we come to see that although we can't change our past, we can discover meaning, purpose, value, connection, resilience, even transcendence in it—and, in fact, we must, if we are to be well and flourish.

3. Because it helps us to move beyond feelings of regret and retribution, and to accept with grace our own, others', and life's inherent imperfections and limitations.

4. Because it shows us how to reorganize our historic record of pain and better use our past to garner strength, rather than resentment and resignation, and to hold feelings of lament and hope at the same time.

5. Because it helps us to understand that our past is far more than "this" challenge or loss—that the same life that causes pain also brings us joy; our past includes happy times, as well as sad times, therefore, it can also be something to seek comfort in.

6. Because it shows us that we all have a worthwhile story that continues to unfold with each passing moment.

And that we must honor that story, with its thorns as
well as petals, and leverage it in healthy ways because
that's truly what will lead us to a better today and
brighter tomorrow.

A BIT ABOUT "STORY"

*Memory is a powerful tool; when it speaks, it tells a story—and
this account often has more influence than historical fact.*

Stories don't only reflect life, they also shape it, which is one reason we often end up becoming the stories we tell about our experiences. This is because stories give us a way to make sense of what
happens in our lives and to prioritize them in our minds. Through
story we form and examine what we believe to be true, and then
we set these truths against others' truths. In listening to stories,
our truths are both reinforced and challenged. In sharing stories,
our realities both solidify and shift. Ultimately, the stories we tell
ourselves and others determine what we remember about the past,
notice in the present, and influence how we approach the future.

Understanding the power of story is essential to *Honor the
Past* because so often we turn a painful experience into what Fred
Luskin, cofounder and director of the Stanford University Forgiveness Project, calls a "grievance story." A grievance story is exactly
what the phrase suggests: a narrative that we construct of a pain-
fully triggering event—in our case lost innocence—which we
didn't anticipate, had no control over, and now feel aggrieved by.

At the heart of a grievance story is that we're interpreting an
event in a predominately personal way and that we blame others

or life for how we feel. In doing so, we spin a yarn that turns us into a survivor, victim, or martyr—one of the *Three Harmful Personas*.

Much of the time this happens beneath the veil of our consciousness. It's not that we want to be miserable. It's more that suffering with a grievance gives us a sense of validation and security.

In the field of psychology, there is the *principle of symptom coherence*. In short, it says that whatever manifestations of pain or symptoms of suffering a person experiences are not a disease or a pathology, as many suggest. Rather, they are adaptive, protective mechanisms, based on mental models about ourselves and the world that we've developed along life's path. Everything from our biology and genes to our attachments as children, to our habits, mores, associations, belief systems, even our nervous system conspires to keep us "safe" through the manifestation of some symptom—like lost innocence's pain or despair.

Many researchers suggest that much of our suffering is not caused by the factual events of what happened to us; rather, by the stories we tell ourselves about what happened. A key part of learning to *Honor the Past* is taking a good look at the story we're telling about our experience. In the coming pages, we'll delve into how best to do that, but before we do, I want to say the following about story. Keep it handy as you consider your own story going forward.

Stories can either empower us or confine us—it's our choice. We can't get rid of our stories, but we can change the way we think about them and how we allow them to influence our lives. When we take ownership of our stories and live by the "right" stories (the Goldilocks principle), we gain that much desired sense of coherence. We also come to see that our stories never climax and never end, even when our bodies eventually do. In this way our stories can be our gift to posterity and so become a part of our legacy. That said, stories are also absolutely essential to our life in the present: stories nourish, empower, and sustain us each day throughout all of life's situations.

It's important to remember that story is not wish-fulfillment gone wild. Yes, we all can rewrite our stories at any point in our lives, but doing so involves understanding and integration of past stories in the present.

HONOR THE PAST—MAKING IT REAL

Bend without breaking. Adapt with hope and confidence. And move forward in life with ease and renewed peace.

The Goal

Our goal for *Honor the Past* is consonance. If you've ever heard a musician hit a wrong note while playing an instrument, you'll know immediately what this means. Lost innocence can throw a big "clunker," as my piano teacher used to call such a misstep, into the beautiful sonata of our lives. The way to regain the harmony is by reconciling our past with both our present situation and expectations for the future. And here is where those kernels of truths will come into play. It's not only that we begin to think about our situation differently; it's that we actually *feel* within us that something has shifted—a puncture in the bubble of pain, a release of suffering's steam—that allows us to open up to our own or the world's goodness once more.

It seems funny to say, but in *Honoring the Past*, we actually experience a sense of peace and understanding that can be felt in a present moment.

The Challenge

The challenge of *Honor the Past* comes down to choice: Are we willing to let go of our pain or suffering? And are we willing to get to the emotional truth that's maintaining it? Are we willing to reset our heart's compass and grow in gratitude for the meaning we've found in what was? If the answer is yes, then it will take some *admitting* and *acknowledging* (more on that soon).

Plan of Action

As I mentioned, *Honor the Past* takes some heart-centered work—which doesn't always come easily. In large part, that's because we don't know how to do so in a way that doesn't make us feel overwhelmingly vulnerable. The good news is that there are some very good techniques to safely "touch the murky places." Some are straightforward; others, at first, may seem foreign or even uncomfortable, but with practice, like anything, they can become second nature.

For each of the time frames of HTC, there will be centering or grounding exercises to get you in the necessary embodied state to engage the thought stimulators, meditations, and practices. There will also be suggested rituals to help you sustain the good work that you've done.

Also, for each time frame, it is good to prepare. Here are a few suggestions:

- ❖ **Don't rush the process.** Take whatever time you need to really delve into that frame in a way that sets you up for success. Drop in when you can be fully present to it and drop out when it becomes too much. The only schedule you are on is your own.

✛ **Queue up "trusted others."** You may want to discuss new insights and experiences with someone else, in addition to processing them yourself. Good support is essential, so be sure to reach out to your inner circle.

✛ **Share the process.** If someone else you know is going through a similar experience, it can be helpful to chat about your progress, challenges, or questions.

✛ **Don't jump ahead to other time zones.** Do them in order H, T, C.

One thing to bear in mind is that HTC is not a substitute for psychotherapy. It can certainly be used alongside any counseling or treatment that you may be receiving, and you may wish to consult your therapist or other professional prior to beginning the process.

If you're ready, let's get started.

GETTING IN THE RIGHT STATE: SPIRIT, MIND, AND BODY

I said earlier that getting into an "embodied state" is helpful before diving into each frame. When people talk about an embodied state, essentially, they are describing a felt awareness of the entire body—all the tactile sensations that flicker and shift like heat lightening beneath our skin and whispering words in a language all their own to affect how we feel and think. It's a sensory awareness that helps us to feel spacious yet grounded.

For *Honor the Past*, I have found centering practices to be a good way in. Centering refers to being in a relaxed and focused state. It's a way to bring calm to our emotions, which is especially helpful when we're feeling something strongly—like the difficult emotions that result in the wake of lost innocence.

There are an infinite number of centering practices to choose from. If you have a preferred one, feel free to use it. If not, or in case you'd like to try something new, here are a few options.

Cellular Breathing

Earlier I mentioned that trying to get my old life back, pre–heart attacks, felt like scrambling to hold onto air—an impossibility, given its gaseous structure. And yet while our hands can't physically grip air, holding onto it and distributing it, through the process of breathing, is precisely what we do at every moment of our lives.

Breathing is the most essential human function, but it's also something we don't often think about because it's a reflex action, meaning it happens automatically. Of course, it may also be because we easily get distracted with the other stuff of life.

I remember when I was in the hospital, recovering from having the stents inserted into my heart. I asked one of the physician's assistants (PAs) what I could do to help myself. "Don't forget to breathe," she told me—and she wasn't kidding. When we're nervous or hyperfocused, we hold our breath. When we're overstimulated, it's difficult to catch our breath. When we try to suppress tears or stifle a strong emotion, our breath becomes weak or irregular. Not only reminding ourselves to breathe, but also breathing deeply can help us immensely.

Deep breathing has many names: diaphragmatic breathing, abdominal breathing, belly breathing, to name a few, and many techniques to do it; *Cellular Breathing* is one.

Cellular Breathing helps you get grounded and stay present by focusing on the pure sensations of natural breath. It's a subtle yet powerful way to calm and get centered quickly.

Start by lying flat on the ground. Place your right hand over your heart and your left hand on your belly. Notice the places where your body is touching the earth. Let these places sink downward. In the stillness, start to notice the rhythm of your breath. Inhale, feel the lungs fill. Exhale, feel the lungs empty.

Notice what happens in your body when you focus on your hands—their weight and temperature—sensations throughout your body, changes in breathing.

Next, focus on the hand on your belly. Feel it rise on the exhale and lower on the inhale. Keep doing this and notice what's happening. Maybe the breath feels cool on the way in and warm on the way out, or maybe your heart has space around it. Imagine a wave cresting and falling, bringing in fresh, clean air, restoring and replenishing the toxins that were being taken out when the wave falls.

When you're ready, start to make some small movements. Slowly roll onto your side. Take a moment, then bring your attention back to your surroundings.

Grounding in Gratitude

This practice is adapted from Fred Luskin's guided visualization for forgiveness. For any process that requires reconciling and emotional learning, it's often helpful to start from a container of compassion and kindness. This is because it helps to hold any pain or distress that may bubble up because of the work.

Start by finding a comfortable place to sit or lie down. If sitting, make sure your feet are flat on the floor. Close your eyes, again if you feel comfortable, and place your right hand over your heart and your left on your belly. Roll your shoulders a few times in both directions, then let your head drop slowly to the front and back and left and right to release any tension.

Next, let your mouth and jaw relax by placing your tongue behind your front two upper teeth. Breathe gently into your belly, letting it expand outward as you slowly take air in and cave in as you push the air out. As you inhale, conjure a sense of goodness—visualize an image, hear a song or voice, imagine a touch. As you exhale, conjure the feeling of safety.

Now, recall people or things in your life for which you are grateful. They could be present in life now. They could have moved away or passed on. They may even be characters in a story or a person from history that you connect with in some way. Allow that gratitude to course through your body, and savor each sensation, however small. Remember moments of kindness in your life—when others have been kind to you and when you have been kind to others. Let those feelings course through your body as well, savoring each one. Lastly, think of a moment of feeling loved and cherished by someone, then remember a moment of you loving and cherishing someone, even a beloved pet. Allow the feeling of love to flow through your body.

Finally, let yourself feel your own goodness. If that's difficult because of a moral injury, then recall a time from your past when you felt that way. Sit with that feeling for a few moments, then let it open into a sense of goodness in humanity. This is the place from which forgiveness and reconciling comes.

DROPPING IN AND OUT OF EMOTION

Exploring each of HTC's time frames tends to stir the pot of emotions, especially the difficult ones in *Honor the Past*. But emotions aren't something to fear or avoid, even the ones that don't feel great. Emotions are inherently neither good nor bad; they're simply messengers. They tell us what's working and what isn't, what's missing and what we need more of, among other things. In this way, each has an important function.

How emotions work is fairly straightforward: some stimulus or signal triggers our brain, which takes about a quarter of a second to identify; then, in another quarter of a second, a chemical is produced that surges through our body, and so forms a brain-body feedback loop.

Each burst of emotion, from signal to when it's broken down and absorbed, lasts roughly six seconds. If it goes on any longer, then we are in essence choosing to hold onto it—to positive or negative effect. This brings us to feelings. Feelings result when we choose to hold onto an emotion, in other words, when we allow an emotion to soak into our brains and bodies, or else when we allow multiple emotions to intermingle. Hence, feelings are more cognitively saturated than emotions; they also last longer.

The key to optimal emotional care lies in recognizing what we are sensing in a moment, gauging its purpose for a given situation, and choosing to hold onto it or let it go. Doing so requires being in touch with our internal landscape. Unfortunately, this is not something that comes naturally, especially to adults; nor is it something we're typically taught as kids, like the multiplication times tables. It also becomes harder to do when we've experienced adversity because, as research shows, traumatic experiences run roughshod over our body, bringing us to the edge of our window of tolerance.

UNDERSTANDING YOUR WINDOW OF TOLERANCE

Everyone has a "window of tolerance," a phrase coined by Dan Siegel, to describe normal brain/body reactions, especially following adversity. The idea is that human beings have an optimal arousal level that allows emotions to ebb and flow. When we experience anxiety, pain, anger, grief, hurt, exhaustion, or shutdown that bring us close to the edge of that window, we are, generally, able to leverage strategies to keep us from leaping out. For some people, especially those who have experienced trauma or chronic adversity, particularly at an early age, this window is drastically smaller, meaning they have less capacity to ebb and flow through challenging emotions and a greater tendency to become overwhelmed and overstimulated. This is because traumatic experiences, like lost innocence, can seriously disrupt our nervous system.

When it comes to emotion, all roads lead to the nervous system—whether it's producing it, sensing it, expressing it, or acknowledging it.

The nervous system (aka the autonomic nervous system) is an involuntary and reflexive, "behind-the-scenes" mechanism in our body that helps to keep us alive. Its job is to regulate how our internal organs function, including the heart, stomach, and intestines.

The autonomic nervous system has two major branches: the sympathetic nervous system (SNS), which mobilizes our body's internal resources to act if there's a threat, and the parasympathetic nervous system (PNS) often called the "rest and digest," "feed and breed," and "tend and befriend" system because it dampens sympathetic nervous system responses and keeps our body in a restorative and resting state. (There is a third branch called the enteric system that is confined to the gastrointestinal tract, but we're going to focus on the first two.)

Typically, both branches play a happy game of "tag you're it," working together to manage our body's responses depending on the situation and need. For instance, if we think we are in a dangerous or stressful situation and need to flee, the sympathetic nervous system will act, dumping a deluge of stress hormones into our bloodstream to give us extra energy to get away; our heart rate and blood pressure soars, our breathing quickens, our muscles tighten, and all nonessential functions, like digestion, become dormant.

Here's where things get tricky. When the sympathetic nervous system is in the driver's seat, with its foot pressed firmly on the body's physiological "gas pedal," the brain's fear circuitry is also operating at full throttle. This is important because it is simultaneously drawing essential resources away from other regions of the brain that control our ability to plan, reason, pay attention, and communicate effectively. In other words, when we're in this "fight or flight" mode, we resort to survival strategies, which is why we tend to act more aggressively and become quick-tempered, avoidant, and withdrawing.

The good news is that when the threat goes away, the parasympathetic nervous system takes back control of the body, slowly pressing our physiological "brake pedal." Heart rate and blood pressure go down, breathing becomes more fluid, muscles relax, and digestion starts to churn. This is because the brain's fear circuitry is no longer sparking out in a frenzy, which means that we are back in "social" mode, being able to think clearly, focus, reason well, communicate clearly, and engage with others.

The bad news is that sometimes—whether it's because of nature (we were born that way) or nurture (we experienced trauma or early attachment issues)—our body's physiological "gas pedal" gets stuck against the floor and we find ourselves careening down Overwhelm Highway. Our senses become heightened, which puts us on "perma-hyper-alert," which causes our reactions to intensify, so that everything seems more severe or doomsday. Other times when the overwhelm gets to be too much and our nervous system becomes depleted, we may start to slow down, shut down, go numb, and dissociate. It's how we survive, but not how we thrive.

Delving into *Honor the Past* can activate difficult emotions and feelings, and so push us to the ledge of our window of tolerance.

But these strong emotions have something important to tell us, and therefore can't be sidestepped. Part of getting at the emotional truth of our past is understanding the somatic story as much as the cognitive one. This requires bringing awareness to the lived reality of our felt sense memory—in other words, paying attention to the "murky places," ripe with sensations, emotions, and feelings bouncing around beneath our skin.

Going back to the "Goldilocks principle." The key to emotional learning—in this case, getting to the emotional truth of our past—is finding the right amount of stimulation to bring into our system. It's kind of like turning the handles on a faucet: too much and we get splattered or soaked; too little and we can't get the job of washing done.

In somatic psychology, the word *titrate* is used to describe how much emotional "flow" we let come into our system's internal reservoir. To titrate our experience is to keep ourselves in an intentional place of choice and safety by opening and closing the tap on our emotions. It's a process by which we slow down our internal response—emotional, cognitive, and physiological—so that we can more effectively process incoming information. It's a skill that can be easily learned and, with practice, mastered. Here are a few tips, for generally expanding your window of tolerance and specifically for when you're intentionally touching the murky places in *Honor the Past*.

Practice Sitting with Emotions

This is a good exercise to do anytime, anywhere. Sit quietly for one to five minutes and pay attention to what's going on beneath the surface. You don't have to go fishing, per se. Just see what bubbles up. As you sense some flames and flickers or feelings, name them. When you're keen to move on from one, don't. Stay with it; be curious about it—how it moves, how long it lasts. And then stay with it a bit longer. If the experience starts to feel too overwhelming, pull yourself out of that sensation by shifting your attention to something external. A great way to do this is the *5-4-3-2-1* method. It goes . . . Name *five* things you can *see* (in your space, out the window). Then *four* things you can *feel* (the warmth of your skin, your feet against the floor, the table in front of you). Then *three* things you can *hear* (cars on the road, birds in the trees, a humming in the ceiling vent). Then *two* things you can *smell* (take a deep breath in). Lastly, *one* thing *good about yourself.* (Note, *5-4-3-2-1* is a good grounding technique for anytime difficult emotions become overwhelming.)

Observe Your Physical Comfort

This one is adapted from Peter Levine's Somatic Experiencing. It is also great for general practice.

Bring your attention to how comfortable you feel wherever you are (best done while sitting in a chair). Take one minute to notice your overall experience. Next, wiggle your toes in your shoes and move your feet on the floor, shifting and adjusting until you feel really connected to the ground. Now, sense your back and bottom on the chair. Notice how it supports it. Notice if it's supporting you or if you are perched to the side or pitched forward. If so, relax into it, and let the chair support you. Adjust until it feels comfortable. Then take a full minute to enjoy being supported and stabilized by the chair. Finally, look around your surroundings and notice something that feels meaningful or restorative—a moving tree outside the window, a piece of art, a happy photo, a calming color, a treasured possession. Allow those restorative feelings to fill your entire being. Then notice how you feel about your overall comfort—physically and emotionally. Take note of what's changed.

Ride the Waves

I mentioned earlier the story about getting tumbled around in the undertow on Martha's Vineyard, and my dad mentioning that part of "riding the waves" was actively seeing one form on the horizon; staying alert but buoyant as it approached; and when it crested, moving with its undulation—rising up in the curve, a moment of immobility at the peak, and eventually sliding back down to calmer waters. This is essentially the heart of titration. Whether it's the process of working through the exercises in *Honor the Past* or anytime difficult emotions begin to form within you, the key is to sense them, acknowledge them, make room for them, and stay with them even as they "crest" and become more intense than feels good, allowing each "wave" to move through—and eventually out of—your body.

When we gain more confidence in our ability to ride the waves of emotion, we start to see our window of tolerance open: we fear and worry less; it's easier to regain calm when we feel overwhelmed; we move more fluidly between difficult and pleasing emotions; we can integrate feeling and thought more effectively; we learn from the messages they carry; and all this gives us a new sense of command or self-mastery.

Our body is the container for all our sensations and feelings. How we interact with it greatly influences our mind and spirit. Many people try to simply think their way out of emotional pain. Although there are indeed some situations that greatly benefit from a cognitive approach, it doesn't universally work. Remember, when we're in states of distress, our rational, higher order cognitive functioning more or less goes out the window because our nervous system is putting pedal to the metal. Whether we're hyped up on anxiety or shut down and numb, or under the influence of any intense difficult emotion, the key to relief lies in regulating the flow of stimulation into our system.

Titration, or dropping in and out of emotion, allows us to open and take in new information while also giving us the necessary space to process that information in a way that is authentic and safe. As you continue onto the following exercises, or anytime you experience a tsunami of overwhelm, try using one of these techniques.

EXERCISES TO *HONOR THE PAST*

The following exercises will help you find those "kernels of truth" or seeds of hope in your experience of lost innocence. Read through each, but don't feel as though you need to answer each one. In fact, don't merely answer them at all. Instead, choose one or two that most resonate with you and that stretch you the most, and respond to those. The ones you choose should make you think in ways you haven't thought before. It can be helpful to have a notebook or journal.

Retell the Past

Literally write the story of your experience of lost innocence. And when I say story, I mean *story*—as in characters, setting, conflict, plot twists, themes, point of view, climax, resolution/outcome, and so on. This is not meant to be a chronology or technical manual. It's also not going out for publication, so don't get hung up on making it perfect. Just include all meaningful information, including who's involved, what occurred before, during, and after the event(s). Describe what you thought about it at the time and how your thoughts have evolved from then until now. Include how you felt, both then and now, as well. Don't hold back or censor yourself; let it fly on the page. Use quotes and exclamation points to give voice to your emotions or ellipses (. . .) when you can't find a word or phrase to capture the felt sense. Be as honest as you can; remind yourself it doesn't matter what kind of light you're casting onto the situation or what kind of light you're casting onto yourself or others. Remember, this is a first-person account (or point of view), so if you find yourself starting to analyze or pretty up the content, stop! This is the time to "drop out"; you're no longer in that embodied container. Try a *Centering Exercise* or the *5-4-3-2-1* method to get back there. When you are back, keep writing the story until you're satisfied that you've captured all essentials.

Give Witness to Loss

Next, when you're ready, get a highlighter and mark individual words or phrases that best capture your experience of lost innocence. When you're done, make a list of them separately, then review. Spend thirty seconds on each one and notice where in your body you feel something—a jolt, an impulse, tightness, heaviness, breathing patterns, a way of holding your posture. Make a note about this as well. Now pay attention to any emotions that bubble up, and then actively try to hold onto each for a few moments. Record what it feels like to hold that sensation. When you're done, put down the paper and pen and notice what your breathing is doing—is it shallow or interrupted; are you holding your breath? If so, you might be "holding onto air" in an unhealthy way. Try one of the deep breathing techniques previously mentioned to get your lungs (and not a negative memory) involved, so that you can return to a place of calm goodness.

Over the next few days, do this same review practice and see what, if anything, shifts.

Deconstruct Your Story

When you've had some space from the story you wrote down (a day or two is best), pick it back up. This time read through it as though it were a novel, not your memoir. There may be the tendency to want to become your own editor; that's not helpful just yet. The point here is to be an observing member of the audience, as much as that's possible. You can also record yourself reading the story and then listen back to it. Sometimes the ear processes things differently than the eye, which can give you a different perspective.

Read or listen to your story once through for content and then again for the sensations that pop up. Drop into those sensations and explore them. Notice what they're telling you—messages these sensate voices are carrying, the meanings of the words they're whispering. Drop out if they become too intense by using one of the *Centering Exercises*.

Now, analyze the story the way a book or movie critic would—be honest, but benevolently so. Ask yourself if you are happy with the interpretations. Are they *fair* interpretations? Have you in any way created a grievance story? Look for signs of one of the *Three Harmful Personas*: note in what ways you might have written yourself as a survivor, victim, or martyr. Notice if you're blaming someone or something for how you're feeling, and record who or what you're blaming them for. Observe the ways in which you might be taking an event or situation especially personally. Notice which characters in the story are getting the most attention; locate who's central to the story and if there is a villain. If you fact-checked your story, would there be any inaccuracies? Can you pinpoint the central argument or theme of the story? Can you bring it down to one compelling summary statement? You get the point.

Next, notice what you're feeling about the story as a whole—if you're bored, confused, bitter, angry, and so forth by it. Drop into those feelings and listen for some meaningful message to come through; make sure to make notes of those as well.

Now, read through your story again—slowly—and ask yourself if you've told any white lies about the story or stretched the
truth about the story. Were there things that you were afraid or
embarrassed to include in the story? Make note (in a different
color pen) of what, if anything, you left out. Notice any sensations
that bubble up here too.

Lastly, observe if your general sense of pain or suffering has
biased your story in any way. Can you now discover or develop
alternative meanings or interpretations of the story of your lost
innocence? Are there new words to include and highlight in your
story? If so, write them down.

Deconstructing our story is a powerful experience because, as
discussed, stories give us a way to make sense of our experiences.
Remember, most of our suffering isn't caused by the literal events
of what's happened to us; rather, it's in the stories we tell ourselves
about those events.

Taking this step back from your narrative to see the ways in
which it might be filtered through hurt or offense is necessary
to fully be able to *Honor the Past*, for it's only in the light of truth
that healthy meaning can be found. And don't be discouraged or
embarrassed if you did stretch or distort things a bit (or a lot)—we
all do it; we're only human.

From here on out, I encourage you to think of this story as
"raw material" or your "rough draft"; no story comes out complete the first, second, even third time around. To rewrite your
story in a way that is *right* and *real* for you specifically, you must
first let in and process the fullness of your experience and consider its impact.

The following exercises are for helping you to acknowledge the realities of lost innocence and its impact on your life. Choose any that resonate. As always, be mindful of what's happening below the surface, and be sure to drop in and out of emotion as necessary.

Honest Grieving: Acknowledging and Admitting

Part of *Honor the Past* is acknowledging and admitting. You might wonder what the difference between the two is. In brief, acknowledging is being present to messages from our mind, whereas admitting is listening with our body. Here is what I mean.

I understood that I had had a heart attack when the ER doctor said the words, "You're having a heart attack." And the severity of the situation wasn't lost on me when I heard that person yelling, "We're losing her!" But it was only when I read my 250-page medical file a month or two later that I was fully able to acknowledge the reality of those events and what they meant for my life going forward. Seeing my name next to words that are so often associated with dire illness and death made my heart skip more than a few beats. And reading various doctors' notes about how very sick I was and the rarity of my condition was enough to break my heart all over again. For a while, I was numb to all that had happened, distracting myself by obsessively managing all my new realities, including the lineup of medicine, cardiac rehab, and new rules, such as no longer picking up my cats or using sharp knives. When I wrote out my own story of what happened, it was chock full of elements of all *Three Harmful Personas*. I also noticed a grievance story aimed smack at life's lack of available information.

When our arm or leg falls asleep, we lose circulation and go numb. So, what do we do? We rub the limb to regain the feeling. As the blood begins to flow and the feeling comes back, we may sense an initial surge of pain, but in time that pain goes away and we can use that limb once again. Honest grieving is much like this.

Let's start with the process of acknowledging.

First, think back to the "first draft" of your story. On a scale from 1 to 10 (1 being the least and 10 being the most), how much do you experience each of the following in connection with it. You can also choose 3–5 that feel particularly relevant and 3–5 that are least relevant.

Anger	Distrust	Rage
Anxiety	Envy	Regret
Apathy/	Fear	Rejection
Indifference	Frustration	Resentment
Resentment	Grief	Sadness
Betrayal	Guilt	Self-criticism
Blame	Hate	Shame
Confusion	Hurt	Worry
Despair	Loneliness	
Disappointment	Powerlessness	

Now, consider how this story draft has shaped and influenced aspects of your life. What is it costing you? What are you sacrificing to keep it going? If all the pain was taken away, how would this story change? What will be lost? And what might be found?

Grievance Scan

Consider:

÷ How have the pain and grievances in your story's "first draft" impacted your life until now—think health, work, intimate relationships, other relationships, finances, contributions in life, and general well-being?

❖ How will these grievances impact your future if they continue?

❖ What are your pain and grievances protecting you from?

❖ What do you have to gain from keeping the situation as it is? What would you lose if it was to resolve or transform, or if you healed and moved forward?

❖ What message does this tell you now?

The Desire Inventory

The Desire Inventory helps you recount how this challenge or loss has directly affected your ability to satisfy the *Six Fundamental Human Desires.*

❖ **Meaning:** How has this challenge or loss distracted you from what matters most in your life? What mattered most in your life before? Does it still? What was the unifying focus of your life? How has this been affected by what's happened?

❖ **Purpose:** What, if any, pathways to the future seem closed off because of this challenge or loss? What detours will you need to take to move forward?

❖ **Value:** What beliefs or principles have been called into question that once helped you to make sense of yourself, others, and the world? Examples include trust, companionship, the belief that you are invincible. Are there any that have become stronger or weaker?

❖ **Connection:** What relationships have changed because of this challenge or loss? What have you done specifically to affect them?

❖ **Resilience:** How specifically has this challenge or loss made you smaller? What resources are you no longer leveraging? What negative thoughts are holding you back?

❖ **Transcendence:** How, where, and with what frequency did you previously find wonder and awe? How has this changed since this challenge or loss? What makes that so?

Taken together, what message does this tell you about how your past is affecting your ability to move forward into new life?

Now let's turn to admitting.

Said the poet Albert Huffstickler, "Let the pain be pain, not in the hope that it will vanish but in the faith that it will fit in, find its place in the shape of things, and be then not any less pain but true to form. . . . That's what we're looking for: not the end of a thing but the shape of it."

Most emotional wounds are based on interpretation, especially those aimed at ourselves, such as "I'm bad," "I'm a failure," "I'm powerless," "I'm inferior," "I'm damaged," "I don't deserve," "I'm not enough," "I'm all alone," "I'm not wanted," "I don't matter," "I'm different," "I'm wrong," "I'm not safe." The list of negative "I" statements that result in the wake of adversity is endless. Fred Luskin describes these statements as "core wounds." Core wounds are those messages we internalize about what a triggering event meant about us.

Now, these messages don't just pop out of thin air in the present; they are often rooted in patterns from the past—from attitudes and beliefs that grew out of previous experiences. "[These wounds are] imprinted into our emotional body," says author and journalist Michael Brown, "before our awareness consciously entered the mental realm, so they are not located within us as thoughts, words, and concepts, but as feelings."

It's essential then when engaging in the process of honest grieving that we not only identify those core wounds about ourselves, but also trace previous times when we have experienced these same feelings. In admitting what these core wounds are, we can bring better awareness to the root of the issue, this time with emotional clarity that will help us to find those much-desired kernels of truth.

Open Your Heart

Admitting requires you to drop into your pain. To do that safely, it's helpful to first get into a place of calm. The *Open Your Heart* technique can help with this. It's a gentle seated posture that opens your chest and throat.

Find a comfortable place to sit—in a chair, on the floor, at the base of a towering mountain; anywhere works. Bring your hands to your shoulders, elbows facing front. Inhale, as you expand wide across your chest. Open your elbows as far as they'll go, and slowly lift your chin. Exhale, as you pull your elbows into the front of your heart and tuck in your chin. Breathe deeply for a count of eight, focusing on your inhalation. Repeat, until you feel something shift. (Don't worry if it doesn't happen right away. Keep going. It will.)

Now, consider what messages about yourself this experience of lost innocence sent. Again, bring your hands to your shoulders and inhale, opening your chest and exhale, pulling in your elbows and chin. As you breathe deeply, notice any sensations wriggling about and what messages are coming through.

Next, consider all the work you've done so far to *Honor the Past*; what emotions and feelings have been most activated? Repeat the technique. Again, as you breathe deeply, notice any sensations and the messages that are accompanying them.

Do the same for each of these questions. Which negative "I" statement ("I'm powerless," "I'm inferior," "I'm damaged," "I don't deserve," etc.) best describes any messages about your experience of lost innocence; note the emotions that accompany it. Then trace that message's emotional lineage: can you recall other times in your life that you experienced the same message and feelings? How early does it go back? As before, breathe deeply and notice the sensations and messages coming through.

Forgive and Flourish

Sometimes our experience of lost innocence causes us to become our own worst enemy. We become survivors, victims, or martyrs. We work against our own best interests. We stop showing up for life and taking responsibility for *our* life. We get trapped in our heads, dwelling on past grievances, personal histories, lost dreams, and abandoned hopes. We allow ourselves to get sucked up in an "existential vacuum," forgetting how to really live—and live *now*.

A key part of trusting ourselves is forgiving ourselves. None of us is perfect, as much as we may wish it or aspire to it. And all of us have regrets. What matters is that you're treating yourself with benevolent honesty—that compassionate clarity that helped you in *Honor the Past*. So, ask yourself now:

 ❖ Are you presently holding any grievance against yourself? Make sure to include any recurring negative "self-talk."

 ❖ How have you not lived up to your own expectations? How has this impacted the negative stories you carry about yourself and your or others' suffering?

✤ What does it feel like not to forgive yourself and carry this burden?

✤ What helps you to survive your mistakes? Who or what supports you in forgiving yourself, having compassion with yourself, and accepting yourself? What works against you?

✤ What resistance do you have to forgiving yourself? Is there anything you need to do before you can? Do you need to apologize or make amends for anything?

✤ How have you learned from your mistakes or missteps? What is the growth opportunity or "kernel of truth"? What promise(s) can you make to yourself *now* that will serve your greater good?

Plunge into the Meaning

Now, take any key insights that you gleaned from the earlier exercises (from your "rough draft," *Grievance Scan*, and *The Desire Inventory*) and sit with them, one at a time. Ask yourself what's going inside as you consider each response. Notice any new messages or meanings that are being conveyed. If at any time you start to feel overwhelmed, say to yourself, "I'm doing well. Just try to stay with the feeling a bit more."

By holding your interpretations and beliefs up to the bright light of truth, their accuracy and trustworthiness come to the fore. In admitting which ones are authentic and which ones are distorted, you are better equipped to find those kernels of truth and open the door to new life.

The goal for *Honor the Past* is consonance—the weaving together of pain and meaning, dark and light, that shows you how every aspect of life has a key role to play in making you who you are. When we dwell on what we lost, we hand over power to the smallest parts of ourselves. When we lament the loss but hold onto the goodness that it brought to our lives, we come to see that while we may have lost the thing itself, its worth lives on within us. Our heart may ache for some time; it may even always ache at certain times, but we must let the ache be a reminder that the same life that took something from us also gives things to us.

As you now identify your own kernels of truth, consider the following:

- What is most *at stake* for you about this challenge or loss?

- How are you being asked to grow?

- What about this situation matters most to you, and how are you going to let it affect you going forward?

- Imagine you're at the end of your life, looking back. How was this challenge or loss an important part of your journey?

- What gifts have you received from the experience that you might not otherwise have received?

ARE YOU READY TO MOVE FORWARD INTO NEW LIFE?

Being able to fully *Honor the Past* may be experienced as a moment of grace. Grace is not discussed much in everyday modern society, given its roots in religion, but grace is actually a beautiful concept. In its simplest form, grace is the experience of feeling that we're blessed (generally speaking) beyond what we might have reasonably expected.

Flannery O'Connor, the renowned American novelist, once said of her characters' torment, "I have found that [it] is strangely capable of returning [them] to reality and preparing them to accept their moment of grace." Whatever torment your experience of lost innocence has brought, the question now is, are you ready to take hold of these kernels of truth, root them safe within the ground of your being, and move forward? Are you ready to fine-tune the "raw material" of your story's first draft and shape it into a more coherent and fulfilling story? Are you willing to make yourself available to a moment of grace—to sense a glimmer of being blessed, not just burdened; to inhale a big fresh breath into the belly of your spirit?

Timing is significant for taking this step. It's not something you do because you "should." That would make it inauthentic, and so unsustainable. You take it because you've felt the shift within because you accepted the grace of those kernels of truth. It's helpful to check in with yourself to see if you're trying to step forward because you think you should, rather than feeling yourself ready. If something in you is resisting, it's best to listen to that resistance and explore it further. Go back to some of the exercises. Try exercises that you might have skipped over. Reread your story and see what emerges. Even if you want to move on, you must only do so when it feels right and real.

Ask yourself now:

✢ On a scale of 0 to 10 (0 being not at all ready, and 10 being completely ready), how ready are to *Honor the Past* and move on to *Transforming the Present?*

✢ If you're not ready to fully *Honor the Past*, record whatever is the resistance and reluctance. Drop into those sensations and notice the images, thoughts, and messages that arise. If those feelings had a voice, what are they saying? What do you need to fully *Honor the Past?*

RITUALS FOR *HONOR THE PAST*

Ritual plays an essential and powerful role in our lives and have long been at the heart of every culture. Rituals give us a way to make sense of the familiar and the unknown. They provide anchor points for finding stability in the midst of change or transition. They give us structure and reduce stress in times of chaos and confusion. They allow us a safe space to reflect on life's events, both small and large. And they help to give us a sense of coherence; the word *ritual* has Indo-European roots that mean to "fit together" to create order. In this way rituals help bring together the past, present, and future; likewise, the body, mind, and spirit.

Honoring the Past is an ongoing process. Remember, having a coherent sense of time means seeing yourself fully in all frames; and this means moving fluidly among them, as needed. The past is no longer something to fear or avoid or get stuck in. The same way you drop in and out of emotion, so too can you—and ought you—drop in and out of time.

If you stand in a tradition, whether spiritual or secular, you may already have some rituals that could help to *Honor the Past*.

You may also benefit from delving further into new practices. Here are a couple for consideration.

Take Root

I've often heard counselors or therapists suggest a *Bury the Past* ritual. It basically goes that you write down on paper or choose something that represents a painful part of your past, and then you literally put that in a container and bury it in the ground. *Take Root* is the flip side of this—and perhaps more in line with *Honoring the Past*. Rather than bury a grievance, plant a seed of hope. One way is to gather seeds that represent each kernel of truth you discovered, and then go out into the world and literally let them take root. Maybe that's a plant in your home, or in a garden on your property. Maybe that's reaching out to one of the many organizations who plant trees in critical forests around the globe and donate one (or more) in your name. There's something very meaningful about aligning your spirit with something grounded in nature.

Let Fly

On the day that a good friend's difficult divorce was finalized, I showed up at her house with balloons—not because she was having a party, and not to minimize the relationship or the path that got her to that point. I brought them for an *Honor the Past* ritual. In Asia and other parts of the world, sky lanterns (also known as sky candles or fire balloons) have been used in various ways to mark important moments in time. They're basically mini hot air balloons, typically made of rice paper, with an opening at the bottom where a lit candle is suspended. To see the release of these off into the night's black sky is stunning, to say the least. Unfortunately, they're not great for the environment. In the spirit of that lifting and carrying off to new places, I brought balloons (environmentally friendly ones and monochrome, so as not to confuse or harm marine or flying animals). On a small paper streamer, I suggested she write down her kernels of truth, along with one thing she will lament the loss over, one thing that was still meaningful now, and one hope she had for the future. We then stood out on her porch, which overlooked the San Francisco Bay, and she let them fly.

If you'd rather not use balloons, or if you can't find ones that don't hurt the environment, you could also just use biodegradable streamers and go out to a high peak or open space on a windy day. There is also the option of releasing a dove, and there are organizations that cater to this activity.

Keepsakes of Courage

This may go without saying, but it goes a long way: having something tangible that serves as a reminder of something meaningful can be incredibly helpful in terms of seeing ourselves in the fullness of time. As I write this, it is the twelfth anniversary of the day I had my first heart attack—which itself is incredibly meaningful. I'm also looking at three keepsakes of courage.

Every year on the anniversary, I pull these items out of a wooden box that holds them the rest of the year. They are my hospital bracelets (from each heart attack) and a biography of Abraham Lincoln. Each hospital stay lasted five days. And each time I was released, I remember taking off the bracelet. It somehow felt like cutting an umbilical cord. Although no one wants to go to the hospital, especially when you're facing death because it reinforces the stakes, it is also the place that is trying to keep you alive. There was something comforting about knowing if something went wrong, there were people and equipment available to help make it right. Going home I was on my own—and if it could happen once, let alone twice, then, in theory, it could happen again. These bracelets are, for me, a keepsake of courage, not simply because they are a reminder of what happened, more so because they represent my willingness to step forward into new life with no guarantees about the outcome.

The biography of Lincoln was a gift from an OR nurse named Dave. He was the first person I met when my local ambulance met the staff at Massachusetts General Hospital and the last person from my medical team to wish me Godspeed when I was released. "Wow!" said Dave with a wink, as the EMTs hustled me from the vehicle's open doors to a bed in the ER bay. "We don't get many around here like you. Do you have a husband?" He was joking, of course, and I looked like anything but "wow"! But he could see the fear in my eyes, and I could see compassion in his. "We're going to take *very* good care of you, I promise," he said with a huge heart-warming smile.

When the second heart attack happened a week later, Dave was there again when I arrived at MGH, this time looking a little forlorn. "Please tell me you are only back to see how you're healing," he said, when the second round of EMTs rushed me from the back of the ambulance to the ER.

Dave was a lifesaver in all ways. He visited me in my ICU room during each shift. He made friends with my family and tried to ease their petrified minds. And on the day that I was to finally leave the hospital after heart attack number two, he brought me a worn copy of a Lincoln biography. "Don't mind the torn edges on some pages," he said smiling, extending his hand to lay the book on my blanketed lap. "I've read it more times than I can count."

You see, when I was having the second cardiac catheterization, when the stents were put into my heart, I had to be awake under light sedation. Apparently, it might have been a little too light because I fully remember a conversation (which isn't common in this situation) that I'd had with Dave about Abraham Lincoln while lying on the OR table with him at my head, monitoring my vitals, and a team of surgeons working furiously behind a blue paper shield that hung at my chest. Dave gifting me that book was a moment of grace. Even though it had lately felt as though the world could give a (insert expletive) about me, this was a much-needed reminder that I had people who cared, loved, and supported me—that I didn't have to go through this experience totally alone; that part of being courageous is acknowledging our vulnerabilities and letting others step in to help.

Keepsakes of Courage aren't merely for nostalgia's sake, although that's not a bad thing. They are reminders of our kernels of truth that help us to be—and stay—well.

There are many rituals from all traditions and persuasions to help us heal from the pains of our past. (See the workbook for *Holding onto Air*, available at micheledemarco.com.) But at this point in *Honoring the Past*, the point isn't just to cleanse the body, mind, and spirit, but also—or rather—to connect these aspects of ourselves to something wholly and holy meaningful.

PAUSE AND APPRECIATE
HONOR THE PAST

Phew. Woo-hoo. Here's to you! H*onor the Past* is an emotionally arduous process. It asks a lot, but it also delivers a lot. At the conclusion of each section of HTC, it's helpful to pause to rest and reflect. Here's how.

Take a few moments to sit quietly without looking at any notes you wrote or work you created during the process of *Honor the Past* to transition to the present. Reflect on the overall experience—how the process generally made you feel. Consider how you felt when you started (e.g., nervous, sad, angry, a racing heart, a heavy heart, fast breathing, tense muscles) and how you feel now that you've finished (e.g., relieved, annoyed, open, curious, hopeful).

PLEDGE OF ACTION FOR
HONOR THE PAST

Honor the Past is a powerful experience, and it might be tempting to conclude, "Okay, now my life will be different and better." I truly hope it is. But it can be easy to fall back into old patterns—we're only human, so it's helpful at this point to make a commitment to positive action. The following are a sample of commitments for *Honoring the Past*. Feel free to add your own. Set a challenge for yourself to try at least two consistently for thirty days. Also, remember to use the *Centering Exercises* previously discussed to help you manage your emotional experience. Note, it takes about a month for the brain to rewire itself and for new practices to take hold.

Optional Committments

I will *Honor the Past* by committing to take the following steps:

1. I will drop into the past by taking time to savor my kernels of truth.

2. I will minimize self-defeating thoughts and behavior, such as "I can't and won't be happy." Or "I'm not and will never be hopeful or happy again." I will find and take comfort in the eternal movement of peace.

3. I will not "catastrophize." I won't expect problems to happen or so-called "bad luck" to curse me. I will remind myself if I'm struggling that I am not eternally damaged, just currently challenged.

4. I will gain a sense of my own narrative coherence by seeing and feeling myself in all moments of time. I will begin to consider how I can weave this challenge or loss into the tapestry of my life.

5. I will practice appreciation and be open to moments of grace.

6. I will look each day to the *Seven Pillars of Resilience* that can best help me to *Honor the Past*.

Like a beloved fable or novel that exists out of time and space, our past, even if only remembered in fragmented, ethereal imprints, is an essential part of our life's story. Therefore, we must respect it, keep it real, discover its truths, and so, integrate it into the fabric of our being. Although we must acknowledge that we can't live in the past, we can and ought to visit it often.

When we *Honor the Past*, we are not minimizing the loss of what was, whether that's a person, our health, security, job, relationship, faith, a belief, an opportunity, or so on. Nor are we not condoning cruelty and unkindness or excusing wrong behavior. We're not trivializing or denying pain. We're simply yet profoundly saying that every aspect of life has a role to play in making us who we are today and who we will be tomorrow. The events we have no control over. The script is ours to write.

CHAPTER EIGHT

STEP 2
TRANSFORM
THE PRESENT

Hold the greatest thing you'll never own . . . this moment.

How much of your time today was spent thinking about something other than what you were doing? Take a guess. Maybe 5 percent; 10 percent; 15 percent, if you were especially stressed. Try 47 percent; no joke, or at least that's what a study at Harvard University reported. That means the average person was "somewhere else," even a little bit, for nearly half their waking hours. The study also suggested that mind wandering has a greater effect on our happiness than income, education, gender, and marital status.

This is a curious finding given how popular "the power of now" has become. Yet perhaps it's not so curious, given how "fragmented, disintegrated, and decoherent," to quote Buddhist scholar B. Alan Wallace, our world has become. It leaves little time to be still, calm, and observant.

Many of the world's wisdom traditions spotlight the impor-tance of living in the present moment, perhaps most notably Bud-dhism. "Only the present moment is real and available to us," said noted Buddhist monk and author Thich Nhat Hahn. "The peace we desire is not in some distant future, but it is something we can realize [now]."

Thomas Merton, the venerable Trappist monk, mystic, and scholar, wrote in a similar spirit that the present has something of the "character of eternity," in which all reality is present at once. He said, "You do not need to know precisely what is happening, or exactly where it is all going. What you need is to recognize the possibilities and challenges offered by the present moment, and to embrace them with courage, faith and hope."

Hinduism, Taoism, Judaism, Islam, and other traditions also encourage us to keep our consciousness alive to present realities; likewise, to make the most of every moment as a gift that will not come again to us in this exact way. Even Sam Harris, the avowed atheist, recognized the value of "now":

> Most of us spend our time seeking happiness and
> security without acknowledging the underlying
> purpose of our search. Each of us is looking for a path
> back to the present: We are trying to find good enough
> reasons to be satisfied *now*... Acknowledging that
> this is the structure of the game we are playing allows
> us to play it differently. How we pay attention to the
> present moment largely determines the character of our
> experience and, therefore, the quality of our lives.

Personally, the sweetest and simplest way I've seen the value of the present moment expressed is by the esteemed children's book author Ruth Krauss in her book *Open House for Butterflies*: "Everyone should be quiet near a little stream and listen."

No matter which path you follow—or don't follow, as the case may be—the point is that the greatest value of the present is that it holds a magnifying glass to all that *is*. The past, while valuable in shaping who we are today, is already over. We can engage it only through memory. The future, though also important, isn't here. It can only be accessed through imagination. The present is "the only time when we have any power," as Leo Tolstoy put it. In other words, we can only act in the present, not in the past or the future. In the present, we can actively choose where to focus our attention. We can also actively choose how we both react to and make sense of our experiences by rethinking what goes into the moment.

WHAT IT TAKES TO LIVE IN THE PRESENT

Mindfulness is the short answer.

It's hard to live in the twenty-first century and not have heard of "mindfulness." In brief, mindfulness is living consciously with alert interest. To fill it out a bit, mindfulness is maintaining the moment-by-moment awareness of our feelings, thoughts, bodily sensations, and surrounding environment through a gentle, nonjudgmental, and nurturing lens. If this sounds like some of the centering and grounding exercises from *Honor the Past*, that's because it is. If you remember from the experience with titration—that is regulating yourself to regain a feeling of safety and kindness when feelings overwhelm—present-moment awareness helps quell the sense of overwhelm.

It used to be that mindfulness was equated to Eastern spiritual practices, such as yoga and meditation. Although both can help to build a mindful muscle, they aren't the only ways. Says Jon Kabat-Zinn, a researcher and author and the founder of mindfulness-based stress reduction (MBSR), "[Mindfulness] is not really about sitting in the full lotus, like pretending you're a statue in a British museum. It's about living your life as if it really mattered, moment by moment by moment by moment."

It's beyond the scope of this book to go into all the ways to build mindfulness and reap its benefits. (See the Further Reading section for a list of books that do.) What can be said, as more and more research shows, is that mindfulness has great physical, psychological, emotional, spiritual, and social benefits. Here are just a few. Mindfulness is shown to boost immunity, improve sleep, reduce stress, and help fight depression. It improves memory, focus, learning, and attention and decision-making skills. Mindfulness increases empathy, fosters compassion and altruism, enhances relationships, increases resilience, even combats bias.

There is a difference, however, between living in a present moment and living within the circumstances of the present. It's a subtle distinction and one not often talked about, but it bears mentioning for *Transforming the Present*.

How long do you think the present is? If you've never thought about it, try it now. It's a rather interesting exercise—one that philosophers, theologians, physicists, psychologists, and neuroscientists have been wrestling with for millennia.

The best estimate from neuroscience is that "right now" lasts about two and a half to three seconds, maybe less. There are also some who see *right now* as an illusion altogether. What's important for us in healing from lost innocence is that we pay attention to *how* we think about the present because how long we understand it to be can influence our outlook on life generally, and our behavior, specifically.

Alan Burdick wrote in *Why Time Flies*, "The present isn't something we stumble into and through. It's something we create for ourselves over and over again, moment by moment." The present then is about our perspective—not only about "now" generally, but also the "now" of each situation in our lives. For instance, when I was in graduate school, I remember thinking that my "present" ended at graduation—only when graduation came, I had to recalibrate that understanding.

Marc Wittmann, a researcher at the Institute for Frontier Areas of Psychology and Mental Health, suggested that our typical timescales for "right now" (e.g., a year, a month, a day, an hour, even a minute) are too long. A few seconds is the range, close to the time it takes to say "now." Interestingly, David Eagleman at Stanford University pointed out that "right now" might actually include bits of the past. That's because our perception is based on sensory inputs that we collect from our body and from the world, and they're not all processed at the same time. For example, a signal from our feet has more travel time up our spine than say our shoulders or lips do. In this way, we're always living a smidge in the past.

And yet we are aware of things that last longer than milliseconds. We watch movies, read books, listen to music, have conversations. One explanation is that we have more than one "now." Wittman outlined three:

1. The *functional now*, the tiny window of time when our brain unconsciously takes in all the sensory inputs

2. The *experienced moment*, a bit longer and more conscious period (approximately two to three seconds) where a single event unfolds and is more psychologically or subjectively felt

3. *Mental presence* allows us to have an integrated experi-- ence, meaning that it's rooted in the global sense of self and erected from the two other "nows." This too provides

a coherent sense of time because it links sensation with
memory to give us a sense of a whole "now"

Much of what we think about time is how we see ourselves in
it. Researchers at UCLA found that the longer people thought the
present lasted, the less likely they were to make decisions that led
to well-being. For instance, if a person thinks that "now" will soon
turn into the future, then they are more likely to take some action
in the present to help shape that future.

Two unhealthy perspectives of the present that Zimbardo identified are the *present hedonistic* and *present fatalistic*. Present hedonistic people "live in the moment," seeking pleasure, newness for
newness's sake, and sensation; they try to avoid pain. They, more
or less, take the notion of "be here now" and turn it into an opportunity to indulge "me here now." Present fatalistic people are more
"whatever now." They feel that decisions don't matter because pre-
determined fate is what guides life; in other words, "What will be,
will be . . . [sigh]."

The same way it seemed funny to say that in *Honoring the Past*
we experience a sense of peace and understanding that can be felt
in a present moment, so too can it seem ironic to say that in *Transforming the Present*—in actively choosing where to place our attention and focus—that we are essentially and crucially influencing
our future.

One of the hallmarks of near-death experiences (NDE) is tran-
scending time and heightened senses. Although my heart attacks
brought me to the threshold of existence, I never officially crossed
over. Interestingly, many people who have had similar experiences—both coming to the edge and crossing over—have

mentioned their senses being hyper-present *after* the event. Whether that's due to some sustained physiological change or unconscious or conscious awareness that life is redolent with stimuli worth paying attention to, given death's alternative, I can't say. But I did notice that this was the case for me.

The first time I really noticed it was on a two-week trip to France.

The impetus for the trip was my ex-in-law's golden anniversary. "Fifty years deserves a trip to Paris," they told us with smiles on their faces. "And we want our family to come along . . . on us." An all-expense-paid vacation to the City of Light and surrounding countryside sounded like far better medicine than the triple blood thinner regimen that had turned me into a walking bruise. I determined to talk to Dr. Kenny.

"Just go easy and don't be stupid," he told me when I mentioned the trip, flashing the warm, knowing smile that I'd come to appreciate. "Take it easy on the hills. Get others to lift your suitcase . . ."

"And enjoy the wine," I interrupted, with a reciprocal smile. "I hear it's good for the heart."

The wine was amazing, by the way. Liquid gold in every sip. But also amazing was everything. Electric. Technicolor. Like Dorothy landing in Oz. I remember one night, taking a boat ride on the Seine. It was freezing—articlike for my thin blood. I was wearing a thick black coat that I had purchased earlier in the day out of necessity, but still I was chilled to the bone—that is, until the boat began pulling away from the dock. The lure of quiet on the upper deck drew me from the hordes below, and when I crested the stairs, suddenly my immediate surroundings and sense of time disappeared. I was overcome by the play of light and shadow; of cold, dark water lapping against the boat; and warm, glowing buildings lining the shore. A few structures erupted in a voltaic rainbow, radiating color from each room, with sound pumping and thrashing and pummeling out onto the river. Chic nightclubs tucked themselves with the discretion of spies in caverns at the water's edge. Crowds drunk on Paris's bubbly spirit cascaded down the cobblestone paths. And in the crescendo, the Eiffel Tower burst big and bright into the night, like an urban aurora borealis. In each of those present moments, any "thinking" me disappeared; there was only a sensing self, whose body overcame the cold as her spirit warmed and settled in.

After Paris, France became something of a pilgrim's journey, only not the typical one that includes well-paved roads that lead to a venerated place or object. Mine was to be a series of moments, with no destination in mind. After the "power of now" (or wow!) that was Paris, I made the commitment to myself to simply let my experience unfold as it needed to and invite whatever feelings, thoughts, sensations, or observations that arose guide me on my journey.

The first "unfolding" came at L'Abbaye de Fontenay, a twelfth-century Cistercian monastery and UNESCO World Heritage Site in Burgundy. It is a grand Romanesque complex of stately and holy buildings, exquisitely tended lands, and a few humble private residences. Strolling the grounds is like one big genuflection. An otherworldly reverence hung in the air like honeysuckle. Again, time seemed suspended; and as I wandered through its labyrinth, I found myself moving much slower to accommodate it. In that space of slow stillness, voices from the past were alive in the present—the sound of ethereal chants and chiming bells; the smell of sweat, must, and ale transported through the centuries. At one point, I came upon a groundskeeper, manually scattering seed on an expansive lawn. In his soil-coated pants and village hat, he paced back and forth, gracefully, and unassumingly, in perfectly straight lines, with a steady but leisurely gait. I paused when I heard a soft sifting rhythm, not unlike a waltz. Over and over the even, regular, and hypnotic little symphony of time and pitch emanated from his boots' soft thud against the ground, the scrape of cloth between his thighs, the flap of a coat tail, the shake of the pouch and its contents, the taking up of each new handful, and the airy final scattering of embryonic seed. His timing was unwavering, like the felt sense within me, both enlivening and enthralling. For a moment, it felt as though my heart was in sync with his—or perhaps it was the eternal heartbeat of life. Whatever it was, it was good.

And finally, Nice.

In the late afternoon on the day before departure, I wandered to the beach across the street from the hotel. The sun was still high, and the Mediterranean azure and calm. For all Nice's teeming energy, for me it was a time of silence. Living consciously with alert interest for the previous two weeks was, even in the quiet moments, a volt of sense. Add to that shifting perspectives about how I thought of my new life "now," and I was a bit tired.

The beach was rocky where I eventually settled down. And I unintendedly created a sort of French-Zen stone arrangement as I considered the realities of what all this meant. France had been a nice getaway after all the change and challenge that resulted after my heart attacks. But the truth was there was no way to stay away from all that occurred. My stents and bruises came with me, as did my story. But somehow experiencing France as things really were—in those series of sensual moments—recast my focus. I no longer sought to escape from feelings or actualities of my new "now." Instead, I wanted to be present and open to them, and to whatever possibilities and opportunities they presented.

I laid back, cradled by a bed of pebbles, and tried to relax. But the tsunami of questions, ideas, and conclusions that hit my mind's shore destroyed any hope of that. I felt myself getting restless, and so turned my attention to stillness. This time it was not a sensation or image that I sought to feel, but the actual "is-ness" of "now," of consciousness, of awareness itself—that vast sea that stretches out between us and everything. I closed my eyes and plunged into that sea. Like the day in the waves off Martha's Vineyard, for a few moments that water seemed dark and choppy; but at last, with fearless focus, I came to feel buoyant and boundaryless. For the first time in many, many months, I was, as my father had put it, "swimming toward the light." And for one beautiful, eternal moment, everything was just as it should be.

TAKING THE PLUNGE

Seneca, the Roman Stoic philosopher, wrote, "Toti se inserens mundo," meaning "plunging oneself into the totality of the world." That totality, you could say, is reality—one that breathes life into our spirit and is experienced in the present moment. Plunging is not always easy, because it requires setting aside certain expectations, assumptions, cravings, and wants, and all the little fears that nag at the back of our mind and pull us towards an inauthentic life. Said Tarthang Tulku, a Tibetan lama, in *Love of Knowledge*, the self wanders the world like an illegal alien, always afraid that its identity will be questioned.

Taking the Plunge requires courageous presence, intentional involvement, embodied participation, not holding back, and saying yes to life every day—in every present moment—come what may.

The present is more than we often conceive it to be. A tiny window of time for our brain to process a signal. An integrated sense of the whole of existence. And everything in between. How we actively live "now"—where we choose to place our attention and focus, what we make ourselves available to, whether we do so from a place of authenticity or fear—will determine how the future plays out.

TRANSFORM THE PRESENT—
MAKING IT REAL

In the end, it is not what you achieve that matters, but rather what you pick up and hold dear along the way.

The Goal

Our goal for *Transform the Present* is trust. Life is deeply complex—and quite simple. We're born. We live. We die. As Jean-Paul Sartre pointed out, "Everything has been figured out, except how to live." He also talked about "living in bad faith," which he described as using life's vicissitudes as an excuse for passivity. Things happen. We can't pretend they haven't or won't. We can't always protect ourselves against them happening. And we can't "live in bad faith" when they do. We alone are responsible for who we are and how we act. We may not always like the options at hand; we may feel like we've been given a raw deal or that the deck is stacked against us or that the system isn't made for us. All of that may have elements of truth. And still, we must live—*now*. The only question is how? How do we learn to trust life again after lost innocence pulled the rug out from beneath us? How do we come to embrace the truth that the same life that brings us pain also brings us joy? How do we accept the realities of what lost innocence means for our life today? How do we say yes to life, affirming that possibility, opportunity, hope, happiness, and peace can still be ours?

Trust is the answer—and this starts with trust in ourselves.

The Challenge

The challenge of *Transform the Present* comes down to fear. As discussed, fear is an innate self-preservation mechanism. But like all machines, sometimes our "self" goes awry. One of those wrenches in our system is rumination. Ruminating is that addictive repetition of a thought—usually a negative, fear-based one—without action or completion. We get trapped in our own heads, cycling through unpleasant or unreconciled experiences of the past or else what might (or might not) happen in the future. At its core, rumination is a heightened state of self-protection. The problem is that when we're in that state, we can't be open to learning new things—which is precisely what we need to do to *Transform the Present.*

Being in the present moment is, perhaps paradoxically, the ultimate protection because fear does not exist there; there is only opportunity and choice. The question is, do we *trust* ourselves to take that plunge? Can we find insight and assert confidence from the clarity that we've found in the present moment? Can we cultivate a courageous heart that speaks with authority and humility? Do we have a resolute reliance on our own integrity? Are we ready to "show up for our own life," to quote the existentialists—to take responsibility for ourselves and our actions in the here and now?

In *Transforming the Present*, it's not only that we begin to think about our identity *now,* but also that we actually feel within us an authentic presence—a stirring of energy, a flicker of faith, a glimmer of desire, a budding from our seed of hope. All this is the bedrock of self-trust and the foundation for our "new home."

Plan of Action

Like H*onor the Past*, *Transform the Present* takes some heart-centered work, only in this case, it's more about cultivating courage than soothing lament.

Perhaps not surprisingly, the Cambridge and Oxford dictionaries both associate courage with fear: they define it, respectively as "the ability to control your fear in a dangerous or difficult situation" and "the ability to do something that frightens one; bravery or strength in the face of pain or grief."

The words *control* and *frighten* reinforce a type of conquering mindset that is seemingly required for one to be courageous. But the word *courage* comes from the Latin *cor*, for heart. I wonder then whether we might reconsider what drives courage. I would suggest that it is not by brute force that we try to conquer our fear, whether that is a physical or cognitive self-flagellation. Rather, it is by tapping into the deep well of emotional strength through a *centering presence*. The heart is, after all, at the center of our body and core to our physical life; even the metaphor of it being the seat of our emotions is fitting.

Cultivating a centering presence allows us to enter into a relaxed, open, and present-focused state. It's a healthy way to take power away from ruminating on concerns and negative thoughts and bring quiet to difficult emotions. When we "clear the murk and calm the waters," so to speak, we can see straight to our spirit's seabed, where true strength and integrity lie. Or as Lao Tzu said, "At the center of your being you have the answer; you know who you are."

The same way *Honor the Past* used centering techniques to get you in the necessary embodied state to engage the thought stimulators, meditations, and practices for *Transforming the Present*, here we'll also use centering. Like before, rituals are offered to help sustain the good work that you've done.

As a reminder, it is good to prepare. Here are a few suggestions:

+ **Don't rush the process.** Take whatever time you need to really delve into that frame in a way that sets you up for success. Drop in when you can be fully present to it and drop out when it becomes too much. The only schedule you're on is your own.

✛ **Queue up "trusted others."** Good support is essential, so be sure to reach out to your inner circle.

✛ **Share the process.** If someone else you know is going through a similar experience, it can be helpful to chat about each of your progress, challenges, or questions.

✛ **Don't jump ahead to other time zones.** Do them in order H, T, C (*Honor the Past, Transform the Present,* and *Craft a New Story for the Future*).

Also, remember that none of the exercises is a substitute for psychotherapy. You may wish to consult your therapist or other professional at any time in the process.

Getting in the Right State of Spirit, Mind, and Body

I said previously that getting into an embodied state is helpful before diving into the exercises. As with grounding, there are an infinite number of centering practices to choose from. If you have a preferred one, feel free to use it. If not, or in case you'd like to try something new, here are a couple options.

Heart Scan: Tapping into Heart Energy

The *Heart Scan* is adapted from Jon Kabat-Zinn's *Body Scan*. It intentionally moves our attention to our heart, attending to any sensations that arise in the present moment. It can last anywhere from two to twenty minutes, and it's easy to do while lying in bed—a great activity to do before sleep.

Start by lying with your back on the floor or on a bed and close your eyes. For just a moment, release all your thoughts and surroundings. Next, bring awareness to the middle of your chest and notice how your heart and lungs feel. Begin to deepen your breath. As you exhale, feel your heart and lungs soften. Allow them to relax. Become aware of your heartbeat and continue to breathe as you notice how you're connecting with it. Spend a few breaths here.

Now, go deeper into the subtle regions of your heart center, beneath the layers of sensations, to a pure and boundless space saturated with peace and glimmers of light. The light may come to you as a color—white, pale pink, gold, blue. But don't force yourself to find one. Just let whatever the experience is . . . be. Continue breathing gently, feeling your breath flowing into and out of your heart. As it does, ask your heart what it desires to say in this present moment? If nothing comes, that's okay. Give it time.

For the next five to ten minutes, just listen without judgment. When it does speak, pay attention to what it expresses—emotions, hopes, wishes, fears, dreams, memories long stored. You may have a flash of feeling—positive or negative. Your breathing may change. You may gasp or sigh or blurt something out. Whatever it is, that is okay. Just keep your attention on your heart center. When you open your eyes, take a few moments to breathe and reorient to your surroundings.

Channel Your Spirit

We talked earlier about spirit being, generally, the animating energy at the core of our lives. This practice helps to get rid of blockages that prevent your spirit from expressing itself and direct its energy into an empowered goal.

Wherever you are (preferably somewhere quiet), do a quick body scan. Start by closing your eyes, breathing deeply and slowly, and moving your awareness through your body, starting at your feet, and working up to your head. Stop whenever you find an area that is unusually tight or sore. Place your mind on these areas, focus your breath, and breathe in and out through your nose. Allow the knots to unravel with each passing moment, releasing into the floor.

Next, imagine all the energy of your spirit flowing into your center. It helps to visualize it—maybe it's a glowing ball or balloon. Now, watch yourself putting all your worry, fear, or negative thoughts in that balloon and then releasing it out into the atmosphere. As you inhale, say "I let . . ." and as you exhale, say "go." If your image was a ball, imagine throwing it far into the distance. If it was a balloon, watch it float up and away. Surrender anything toxic that is blocking your spirit's energy from coming through. Imagine your center filling with calm presence and strength.

On your next inhalation, consider your "kernels of truth" and think of something new you want to realize—a goal, a vision, a purpose. Use positive "I" statements to describe it, such as "I will . . ." or "I can . . ." and channel that spirit again into your center, feeling its sensations pulsing, tingling, and glittering beneath your skin. You can also just repeat one meaningful word to yourself; for instance, consider "alive," "journey," "progress," "trust."

EXERCISES TO
TRANSFORM THE PRESENT

The following exercises will help you "take the plunge" into the present, choose where your attention and energy must be "now"—after your experience with lost innocence—so that you can say yes to life again. Read through each exercise, but don't feel as though you need to answer each one. In fact, don't merely answer them at all. Instead, choose one or two that most resonate with you and that most stretch you, and respond to those. The ones you choose should make you think about new things or in ways you haven't thought before. Again, it can be helpful to have a notebook or journal. (For more exercises, see the workbook for *Holding onto Air*, available at micheledemarco.com.)

Turning Away from Fear's Voice

As mentioned earlier, fear does not exist in the present, only opportunity and possibility. Sometimes, however, the way we deal with our fears affects our ability to "be here now." So, let's now be present to fear.

Consider how fear interacts with your experience of lost innocence. Feel free to engage only the questions that most resonate.

- ❖ What daunting or discouraging messages from past adversity do you carry with you now? How do they affect how you feel about the future?

- ❖ What stories are unresolved or left hanging because of this challenge or loss? Who or what do you need to confront to trust yourself, others, or life again, and move forward?

- ❖ What bonds or connections do you miss out on by not forgiving yourself or someone else?

Now, consider how fear generally affects your life.

- ❖ When does fear most inhibit or block something important to you? How does it distract you from what matters most?

- ❖ What does fear whisper to make you feel less than who you are?

- ❖ In what ways does fear make you sever ties, erect borders, or prevent growth and connection?

✣ When does fear make you ignore your "inner tug"—your soul's call to act as you ought?

✣ What beliefs do you hold that are based in fear?

✣ What is the most significant illusion in life that fear made you think about yourself was real?

Finally, consider fear's lasting influence on you.

✣ What, ultimately, is your *greatest* fear?

✣ What is the *primary* way that fear has negatively impacted your life? When and how has it taken you off guard?

✣ What is fear's specific message to you?

And now consider *your* influence over fear.

✣ If this fear were no longer a part of your life, what would be different? What would you have to give up or let go of? Who or what would you have to forgive or reconcile? Who or what would you have to trust?

✣ What now is your specific message to fear?

After you have quietly contemplated these questions, continue to sit, first bringing attention to your breath, then allowing your attention to focus on your heart. What's it doing? How is it moving? How is your core holding onto air?

After a few moments, recall an experience that fills you with gratitude, love, tranquility, or trust. Sit with that recollection as you begin to experience peace and empowerment *now*. Slowly, bring yourself back into your surroundings, attempting to bring with you that sense of peace and empowerment.

	AGREE STRONGLY	AGREE	DISAGREE SOMEWHAT	DISAGREE
I am beginning to have a clear vision of my life going forward that I can articulate.				
I have good command of my emotions.				
I don't feel dependent on others for my happiness or success.				
My experience of lost innocence no longer haunts me.				
My future doesn't scare me or make me anxious.				
I do things for myself or others because I'd like to or ought to, not because I must or should.				
I know how to set healthy boundaries and live by them.				
I can—and do—abide in the present moment.				
It's getting easier to restore and repair myself when I'm pulled back into pain or concern.				
I am ready to craft a life for the future that satisfies my desires and reflects who I am today.				
TOTAL				

Spirit Wellness Assessment

Spirit Wellness Assessment

At this point it is helpful to gauge how far you've come. The following questions will help you take stock of your present state of spirit wellness. If you answer eight or more as *Agree* or *Strongly Agree*, then your spirit is doing well. If you scored seven or below, then you might want to work on it a bit more.

COMING TO TRUST

The first time I was alone after heart attack number one, literally, number two occurred. My ex-husband had left me on my own to grab a few groceries at a local store and, while talking on the phone with my mother, the elephant stepped back onto my chest.

Looking back, I wonder if I associated aloneness with the possibility of a third heart attack—or more. If I'm honest, I think there is a good a chance I did because for a while, post–heart attacks, I really wanted someone to be with me or at least to be in relative proximity. But I am also an only child who has always enjoyed her solitary time, and as I grew stronger in the months that followed, old patterns started agitating my spirit. *I need space*, I griped one morning when I woke up to one cat licking the top of my head while the other was pushed up tight against my side; at the same time, a phone was buzzing on the end table next to me, and a lawnmower was angrily burping up a branch.

I had been holed up in my house for nearly a year, reflecting on all that had happened, revisiting my past and reconsidering certain aspects of my present situation. I had talked to family and friends daily, even saw them daily. And it was wonderful and helpful. And I was, and still am, eternally grateful for having people to support me. But there comes a time when we need to start supporting ourselves—to "show up for our own life," to take responsibility for the story we are living.

That morning was nearing the year anniversary of the first attack. With the sweet smell of cut grass pouring in through the open windows, it struck me that the past year's calendar had been flipped to the point of reversal. After enjoying a wonderful spring in the peak and prime of life, it closed with two life-threatening blows to my being. Summer, as it arrived, had felt more like a cold, dark winter—both in my body, with my thin blood, and in my spirit. Autumn would follow with a hesitant but budding spring as I found ways to "touch the murky places" and grieve what I'd lost in healthy ways. And winter, bitter and gloomy as it can be in New England, would surprise me with kernels of truth and seeds of hope that bore fruit like a bountiful summer.

As a new spring began to unfold, I too felt a blooming. I was growing in poise with my present situation. I had accepted the reality of what lost innocence meant for my life *now*. Pain had been slowly morphing into empowerment. I was finding new ways to satisfy my desire for meaning and purpose (and the other four desires). I could move more fluidly through difficult emotions and more agilely between thoughts. And I continued to hold onto, for dear life, those kernels of truth I had found—because those kernels centered me in a new present. All of this was great; don't get me wrong. But something still felt disjointed, missing.

The roots of restlessness run deep. And sitting around wasn't helping; neither was continuing to talk to myself and others about how I'd grown. My spirit needed real movement, as Thomas Moore put it. It needed to detach from its current surroundings and, alone, run through the wilds, holy compass ready—only where it ended up was anyone's guess. I needed space to connect with something—or reconnect something—that I still couldn't quite put my finger on.

Wilderness is the place where the Great Spirit or God speaks, so tradition tells us, in a language only decipherable once you enter it—and if you actively listen. At that moment, I was willing to go to the ends of the earth to hear what it had to say. Because such an endeavor would require a lot of planning, I opted for the next best thing: World's End.

There are many World's Ends in the world. The one I was heading to was a state park on a winsome wooded, shoreline peninsula in Hingham, Massachusetts, about an hour and a half south of my home in Newburyport. I had been there a few times before, one time that carried special meaning. And because it was far enough away, without being too far, should something go wrong, it seemed a good bet.

It was overcast when I got into the car, with little more than a North Face shell, a water bottle, my phone, and my nitro. (Nitro, or nitroglycerin, in tablet form treats angina or chest pain when the heart is not getting enough blood flow. The small, cylindrical bottle that I'd been prescribed post–heart attacks "just in case" now went with me everywhere.) I remember getting to the end of my street and pausing, like Samwise Gamgee did when he got to the edge of the Shire in *Lord of the Rings*. Only, I'd crossed this threshold hundreds of times in the past; still, somehow this time felt more profound.

When I pulled off the highway sometime later and headed down the narrow road that led to the parking lot, the sky was drizzling. I was glad for it because it meant that there would probably be fewer people there. It was also the middle of the week, which thankfully, upped those odds. And it seemed I won the lottery because, when I pulled in, there wasn't another car or person to speak of.

I had forgotten the way the land ebbed and flowed into each other—like an hourglass, slightly squashed and askew. The mist hung over it all, muting the verdant trees and grass drumlins, but not in a way that felt sad; more like it was gathering the land in its arms. When I had been there before it was a glorious sunny day, with light twinkling through the trees, casting shadows on the old, carefully carved carriage paths. If the Great Spirit had spoken on those earlier trips, had I been listening, perhaps its voice would have had the sound of chimes, a gleeful inspiration that all is good and would be well.

But glee wasn't in the air just then, although something was. I usually walk with headphones, sound streaming that mimics my mood. But as I passed over a wooded bridge and wound my way deeper into the land, I unplugged. How could I hear what the wilderness had to say if I wasn't actually listening to it?

The smell of ocean and marsh intermingled with the musk of a stand of red cedars that I had stopped beneath. The giant trees were swaying gently toward one another, as if sharing some great secret. I wondered what that secret was, like a child being left out of a circle of trust. Then the whispering winds got involved, lending their voice to the conversation. Even some gulls decided to weigh in with an opinion. And still, I could not take their meaning.

After many hours of strolling in solitude, I was starting to get hungry, but in my haste to get out that morning, I hadn't brought anything. I contemplated heading back to the car and leaving, when some outstretched passerine as white as snow went soaring overhead. It was like standing beneath a B52—wings spanning forever, banking gently and with poise, only its slender and tapering body gave off an ethereal air.

I couldn't believe what I was seeing—not because it was a stunning sight to behold (though it was); rather, because it was a crane or great egret—my "animal spirit" that had visited me when I came home from the hospital after heart attack number two. I remembered peering out my office window, which overlooked a marsh, waiting, watching for a glimpse of that sacred bird. To my joy, he returned often, soaring in, long and low, and then out, high and with grace, giving me glimmers of hope.

Like that day I first saw his relative in the marsh across from my house, the great B52 crane at World's End kept circling and then leaving. I don't remember how long I stood there transfixed. I do remember someone telling me that watching or listening to wild places removes us from time, from our own intentions and limitations. It certainly felt that way to me in that moment; it was as if the human spirit had no limit, including my own.

The trees and the wind were still holding their secret council, but it was the crane's silent soaring that spoke to me. I started walking down the path in the direction he was heading, and when he turned and lifted higher, I quickened my step. He flapped his wings, and the next thing I knew I was jogging. And as he soared off over the harbor, I broke out into a sprint. In the drizzling mist, with my hood up over my head, in wet jeans, and slamming the ground in my old, rubber Wellies, I was running—literally, through the wilds, holy compass oblivious.

"Don't listen for a single sound in nature," I once read, "just listen to that space." In my life, fewer sounds in the space of that moment have been so resonant. I ran and ran, slowing my pace, not because I was worried about my heart exploding but because I didn't want to stop—ever. I could feel the nitro container bouncing around in my pocket. I could feel my heart pounding beneath my shirt. I could feel the diurnal rhythms of the setting sun; and the rhythm of all life's stages; and the rhythm of the cycles found in the wilds, whose heartbeat syncs with our own when we finally pay attention.

I slowed to a halt when I came to the water's rocky edge. I couldn't get air into my lungs fast enough—there was none to hold onto. *Did I push it too hard? Is it happening again?* These had been the questions plaguing my mind for many months. But in that moment, my mind was empty. I intentionally slowed my breath, again, listening to the rhythmic sound of that space—the rustle of swaying trees, the wind, and gulls, me finally deciphering their secret language: "Why walk when you can run?"

For the first time since I arrived at the ER nearly a year before, ashen, and unable to catch my breath, I could breathe—in one transcendent, unified, fully embodied, sacred breath. Spirit, mind, and body in lock-oxygenated step, filling me up, allowing me to trust, making me come to life—bringing me, finally and fully to new life.

All the ride home I kept saying, "Yes!" The same way something in me shifted in *Honor the Past*, it had again. Even though doctors said that it would be okay to start exercising with a little more verve than a stroll, I had been leery. My body had betrayed me, not once, but twice in the form of two heart attacks. In what possible universe would I think that it wouldn't betray me again, especially if I was exerting it? But as I then considered it, perhaps my body hadn't actually betrayed me. After all, it did its job by signaling something was wrong—indeed, very wrong; indeed, dying. It was fear that convinced my mind that water could wash away the pain in my chest that first morning in June when I awoke to the elephant on my chest. It was fear that also made me turn around in the hospital parking lot and leave, despite my skin being the color of a corpse and back pain like an assailant had struck me with a pipe, keeping me from getting the medical care I needed for another seventy-two hours. It was only a suffocating yet resilient spirit that finally said, "Enough is enough."

Perhaps it was *me* who had done the betraying. I had let fear convince me that my body couldn't be trusted when what it was doing was precisely trying to help. It was sending me a very clear message that it couldn't manage on its own, not because it didn't care or was weak but because some things in life are simply beyond our control. Doing anything that comes from an excess or disproportionate place of fear has the futility of trying to hold onto air with our hands. When we come from a place of trust or faith—of that oxygenated, embodied state; lockstep, body, mind, and spirit—then there is no mountain we can't climb, no river we can't cross, no desert we can't traverse, and no wild through which we can't run.

The ride home was quiet and direct. Turning off the exit in Newburyport, I was still in that awe-filled glow. But as the land and trees got denser, and as I approached my road, a rumbling started churning in my belly. When the stone wall at the bottom of my property came into view and I looked up at the grassy, rolling hill and finally to my house, the rumbling quieted, and a bit of emptiness replaced it.

Why is this happening now, of all times? After all that opening and trusting and wonderful insight at World's End? Why am I suddenly feeling a little sad?

The blossoming fruit and floral trees rooted in my land. The family of ducks were floating peacefully across the little pond. There were views of cows grazing, sleeping, and scratching their backs on a wire fence. There was marshland, home to my new friend the crane. The neighbors' son was wielding a surging hose against his sister. My home—the place where I had created so much, confronted so much, and nearly lost everything, now somehow looked different.

I still couldn't deny its beauty, and I felt proud of all the work I had done to make it mine. But the umbilical cord had been cut.

"It's too much." I blurted out.

The passing of my old life ushered in new clarity. Everything about this house looked and felt too big—like Goldilocks in the "Daddy Bear Chair"; a wrong fit. As I looked around now with contented detachment, it struck me that this reality was no longer my life. Slowly, perhaps even unconsciously, I had adapted to the idea of life without kids—that maybe I was meant to "birth" other things. I wasn't ruling the out possibility, but nor was it now a pressing need as it had become in the months prior to my heart attacks. This house, both in size and symbol, represented a different dream and life. I was glad to have had it, but at that moment, I felt that possibly, I was ready to let it go.

Putting down roots was something I had long desired. Maybe that's because when the most consistent thing in your life is the ubiquity of CVS or Starbucks, then you know something has to change. Maybe it was also because I felt the benefits of having had a childhood with roots. But roots are not child dependent, and perhaps also not location specific. Even a tree can be transplanted, so long as the root ball is intact. Maybe the root ball for human beings comes from that enduring and centering energy of our spirit—the one that feeds on possibility and hope and provides the strength and confidence to make change when it is time.

I got out of the car and walked up to the side door of my house. Peering through the checkerboard of small windows, I smiled, remembering wrestling a Corian gorilla sink through it a week before my heart attacks.

Maybe it really was time to move on to *Craft a New Story for the Future*.

ARE YOU READY TO *CRAFT A NEW STORY* FOR THE FUTURE?

When we *Transform the Present*, we trust ourselves that in "plunging" into the present, with focused attention, mindful courage, intentional involvement, and embodied participation, not holding back, our eyes—and hearts—will open to new possibilities and opportunities that will continue to move our lives forward in meaningful ways.

Ask yourself now:

+ On a scale of 0 to 10 (0 being not at all ready and 10 being completely ready), how ready are you to *Transform the Present* and move on to *Craft a New Story for the Future?*

+ If you're not ready to fully *Transform the Present*, record whatever is the resistance and reluctance. Drop into those sensations and notice the images, thoughts, and messages that arise. If those feelings had a voice, what are they saying? What do you need to fully *Transform the Present?*

RITUALS FOR
TRANSFORMING THE PRESENT

As with *Honoring the Past, Transforming the Present* is an ongoing process, for which ritual can help. Remember, having that much-desired coherent sense of time means seeing yourself fully in all frames. And this means being able to move fluidly between the frames, as desired. The present no longer needs to be something to fear, avoid, indulge, or give up on. The same way you drop in and out of the past, so too can you—and must you—drop in and out of "now."

You may already have some rituals that could help you to continue to *Transform the Present*. You may also benefit from delving into new practices. Here are a few for consideration.

Preluding a Moment

There are some moments in life that we know about in advance, such as a marriage, birthday, birth, a big move, an important presentation, or a cherished holiday. Often, these massive meaning moments carry stress in the lead up, precisely because they are so significant. But there are other transitional moments that we too can anticipate: a meal, shifting from work to personal time or vice versa, putting kids to bed at night, the coming of the next day. Taking a moment to reverently bring awareness to what is about to happen, whether it's in the big moments of our lives or something as small as awaiting the morning's sunrise, can help us orient, ground, calm, and focus in the moments leading up to it. It can likewise deepen that moment's significance when it does finally occur.

Candle lighting or incense burning is a common practice. Listening to a piece of meaning music is another. Quiet contemplative time to get centered, bathing or submerging yourself in water, journaling, planting or toiling in the soil, doing some physical activity with intention and reflection, praying or chanting, even just a moment's pause are still others. Essentially, it can be anything that creates a sacred space or threshold for a transition or meaningful event.

Habits of the Heart

This is an embodied ritual examination of sorts that is five steps and is best done in the evening before bed.

Find a quiet place. Begin by bringing your attention to wherever you are. Pause to take a few slow, deep breaths; become aware that you are entering a meaningful or sacred space. Take a moment to feel the stirrings in your body and spirit—feelings, urges, movements. Sit with them. Honor them. Thank them.

Next, *shift your attention to what the stirrings are saying*—what are they asking of you now. What did they ask of you that day? Note this to yourself.

Now, *take note of what you're especially grateful for at that moment*—an event that took place, the love or support you received, courage you mustered, the gift of another day. Focus on the feelings that arise; allow them to flow within you.

Then *consider when you felt joy that day, hope that day, trust that day.* Drop into that sensation and sit with it. What challenged or concerned you that day? Again, drop in and explore. When that day did you pause and take a moment to hold onto—and release— fresh air? Consider what that felt like.

Lastly, *consider the spirit with which you want to enter tomorrow.* Sit with that spirit as you continue to wind down or drift off to sleep.

PAUSE AND APPRECIATE:
TRANSFORM THE PRESENT

Phew. Woo-hoo. Here's to you! *Transform the Present* takes courage. Like *Honor the Past*, it asks a lot, but also delivers a lot. Again, it's helpful to pause now to rest and reflect.

Take a few moments to sit quietly without looking at any notes you wrote or work you created during the process of *Transform the Present*. Reflect on how the overall experience made you feel—how you felt when you started and how you feel now that you've finished.

PLEDGE OF ACTION FOR
TRANSFORM THE PRESENT

Transforming the Present is an empowering experience. As with the other frames, it might be tempting to conclude, "Okay, I'm good. I got it." I'm hopeful you are in a more expansive and confident place than when you started. But as with anything in life, it can be easy to fall back into old patterns, which is why it's helpful to make a commitment to positive action.

Following are sample commitments for *Transforming the Present*. Choose at least two and try them consistently for thirty days. Feel free to add your own commitments to the ones listed. And remember, it takes about a month for the brain to rewire itself and for new practices to take hold. Also, remember to use the *Centering Exercises* previously discussed to help you manage your emotional experience.

Optional Committments

I will *Transform the Present* by making a commitment to take the following steps:

- ✢ I will actively live "now." I will mindfully choose where to place my attention and focus and choose how to react to my experiences.

- ✢ I will practice active embodied listening by taking time to listen to my body—to hearing and feeling what is going on. I will speak with benevolent honesty and disarm the inner critic.

- ✢ I won't jump to conclusions that are based in fear, knowing that they may not be accurate. I will try to recognize when I am distorting a situation.

- ✢ I will take care of myself. I'll take a break when needed or get active when bored. I will give myself simple pleasures, neither in scarcity nor excess. I will support myself in a time of need the same way I would a close friend.

- ✢ I will respect others' differences and be willing to compromise without compromising myself.

- ✢ I will adapt the core me to a new tomorrow. I will redefine, as necessary, the way I see myself, my relationships, and the world. I will hold onto long-held beliefs and principles, so long as they still feel *right* and *real*.

When we transform something, we evolve one thing into another. What's important to remember is that the thing that once was does not simply go away; a seed no longer looks like a seed once it's planted and in full bloom. It's "seed-ness"—its essence—remains embedded in the new growth.

When we *Transform the Present*, we grow our pain into power, into poise, and into possibility. While we acknowledge we may not be able to change our past, we can still act in the present—that it's "the only time when we have any power," as Tolstoy put it. *How* we act is the only issue at hand—fearfully, ragefully, and apathetically, or else confidently, gracefully, and courageously; the choice is ours.

Our most significant life experiences honor endings and beginnings—a rite of passage from one state to another. Lost innocence is one of these experiences; in fact, it's the epitome of existence. We are all, each day, each year, each decade, each disaster, each triumph, each present moment, experiencing something new that challenges or chips away at some old way of thinking or being. Sometimes these moments pass without our awareness. Other times they completely throw off our awareness, so much so, as in my case, that the Gregorian calendar got entirely turned upside down.

These moments, particularly the painful ones, are marked by a threshold, an opening where we stand presently placed and can see both backward and forward—an open door where the past, present, and future all coalesce, allowing us to feel for a brief yet eternal and existentially settling moment what was, what is, and what still can be. Our awareness of this threshold reflects our inner readiness to move from the once known, to the *is*, to the yet to be known.

Let us now engage that unknown.

CHAPTER NINE

STEP 3

CRAFT A NEW STORY FOR THE FUTURE

We are often our own worst enemy but are always our best possibility.

None of us is born thinking about what the future holds and yet we are born with the ability to "pre-experience" it through our imagination. This future-minded superpower, as some consider it to be, is called "prospection." It's a skill that human beings developed to a distinct degree, however, we aren't alone in having it; even dogs get excited at the appearance of a leash or a cat at the sound of a can opening.

One of the primary functions of prospection is that it influences how we act. As discussed in *Transform the Present*, thinking about ourselves in the future helps us decide what to do "now." In fact, research shows that people who feel closer to their future selves are more likely to make wiser decisions, achieve their goals and aspirations, and have better mental health and relationships. For instance, a 2014 study found that looking at realistic computer-generated images of a person's possible future appearance made them more likely to contribute to their hypothetical retirement savings.

Researchers alternatively found that flawed prospection, such as overestimating risk and having more pessimistic beliefs about the future, could be an underlying driver of depression. On the flip side, those who have healthy prospection treat others better. A 2018 study also showed that people were more willing to help someone in need if they had previously imagined the scenario more intimately, such as the event occurring in a familiar place. A further study with volunteers for Hurricane Katrina's relief efforts found those who imagined the positive consequences of their help had a more rewarding trip.

In this way, the stories we tell ourselves about the future can be as influential as the ones we tell about the past. They too can either empower or confine us—it's our choice. When we take ownership of our stories, live by the "right" stories, and connect the stories from the past to the future, we gain that much desired coherent sense of time.

LOST INNOCENCE
IS A NESTED STORY

Our story of lost innocence is a story within a story; in fact, it is a story within a series of stories that make up the story of our lives. To craft that larger story, we must first rewrite a new one for that painful experience.

We talked about how the narrative we recorded from *Honor the Past* was "raw material," a "first draft." Well, now it's time to turn that narrative into something more formal, more *right* and *real*—a story that leverages those kernels of truth and seeds-turned-fruit, and documents how our pain has turned into empowerment. It is a story that tells the *Hero's Journey*, as Joseph Campbell called it—from the "ordinary world" that was once our innocent life; through the "call to adventure" or the cry of pain when a part of it was stolen; through our "refusal to heed the call" because sadness and suffering wouldn't let us accept its reality; through "crossing the threshold" and mustering the courage to charge into the dark uncertainty; to being "tested" by our emotions and then entering the "innermost cave" of our greatest fears; having to face their "ordeals" and coming through it all with grace and presence; and finally, "rewarding" ourselves by catching our breath and holding onto some healthy, life-giving air; to finally "journeying home," wherever and however we define that, with new wisdom, opportunity, and peace.

Craft a New Story for the Future is not about creating a make-believe tale that pretties up or glosses over the "bad bits," nor is it about wish fulfillment gone wild. It's simply telling the experience of lost innocence from your expanded, coherent perspective. It means mindfully putting words to a story that is *true for you*, in a way that is benevolently honest and grounded in hope.

CRAFT A NEW STORY FOR THE FUTURE—MAKING IT REAL

High or low, right or wrong, it's all true.

The Goal

Our goal for *Craft a New Story for the Future* is integrity. "Integrity" is derived from the Latin word *integritas* meaning whole or complete; it's related to *integrate* or bringing together. And bringing together all parts of time in a "whole" story, soundly and authentically constructed, is exactly what we're going to do.

The Challenge

The challenge of *Craft a New Story for the Future* comes down to desire.

Often when we think about our future story, we do so from a place of need or want. Remember, needs are those things necessary for our survival and wants are what we think we'd like to have to enhance our lives. On the needs side, when we consider how the future fits into our life's story, fear can seep back in and grab hold of the pen, forcing our hand to spin a yarn that keeps both our horizon small and us acting only on what we need to subsist. On the wants side, it's just the opposite: our egos can seize authorship, and we start fantasizing about all the nice-to-haves, would-look-goods, and we-deserves. Although it can be fun to daydream about winning the lottery, money can't buy meaning, nor will the reverie support us in our later years.

Craft(ing) *a New Story for the Future* that has integrity must be rooted in desire because only desire has the potential for true joy and positive intention for future outcomes.

Plan of Action

Like each of the other time frames, *Craft a New Story for the Future* takes some heart-centered work. At this point, it might be more exciting than painful. And given all the good work you've done in the preceding chapters, managing it may now come naturally. But life being life, and insight being insight, even at this point emotions can flood or surprise us. So, it's important to use the grounding techniques from earlier to help you drop in and drop out as necessary. There will also be some additional techniques in the pages that follow, as well as rituals at the end to help you sustain the work that you've done.

As always, it is good to prepare:

* ✢ Don't rush the process. The only schedule is your own.

* ✢ Queue up "trusted others." Good support is essential, so be sure to reach out.

* ✢ Share the process. If someone else you know is going through a similar experience, it can be helpful to chat about each of your progress, challenges, or questions.

As a reminder, HTC is not a substitute for psychotherapy. It can be used alongside any counseling or treatment that you may be receiving.

If you're ready, let's get started *Crafting a New Story for the Future.*

Getting in the Right State: Spirit, Mind, and Body

As earlier, getting into an "embodied state" is helpful before diving into the exercises.

Integral Energy

This exercise is adapted from Aikido, meaning "the way of harmonizing energy." It is a Japanese form of martial art that leverages momentum and resistance to deflect rather than overpower one's opponent.

Start by finding somewhere comfortable to sit, so that your feet are connected to the ground. Exhale a long, even breath and, as you do, visualize that breath weaving down into the earth, as roots would a tree, grounding you. Next inhale and imagine the breath cascading over you from above, like a cleansing waterfall.

Feel it washing away any pent-up stress, any toxins floating around inside. Relax, as you concentrate on your vertical core. Roll your shoulders back; stretch your neck up; allow your chest to widen. Feel integrity with this dignified posture.

Now, sense the space around you. Imagine a color or your spirit radiating in waves from your body in all directions. See yourself at its center.

Feel the weight of your body resting into the earth beneath you—your arms, legs, feet, jaw all supported. Then feel the lightness of your spirit in the air above and around you. Notice what it feels like to be supported by all these life-sustaining elements.

Now, reflect on each of the six desires: meaning, purpose, value, connection, resilience, and transcendence. Allow your mind to ask your spirit and body what would it feel like to have more of each? Picture yourself doing something that brings on those feelings. Savor the experience.

Accordion

This technique is adapted from Quigong, a centuries old mind-body-spirit practice that balances our essential energy or vital life force (Qi) by integrating posture, movement, and breathing. By using your hands like the bellow of an accordion or a bicycle pump, you can feel the flow of the force.

Start by closing your eyes halfway. Empty your mind and let your attention fall to your palms. Allow your breath to become slow, easy, without force, as though you are in the very lightest trance.

Next, bring your hands together, palms touching and fingers pointing upward. Slowly move your hands, keeping your palms aligned. When they're about twelve inches apart (or the width of your shoulders), slowly bring them together, using the least amount of effort possible. You will be compressing the air between them like an accordion. Feel a warm or tingling sensation in the middle of your palms.

Continue moving your hands slowly back and forth, varying the range and the direction of the bellows—horizontally, vertically, and diagonally.

EXERCISES TO *CRAFT A NEW STORY FOR THE FUTURE*

The following exercises will help you write the story your life desires to tell. Read through each, but don't feel as though you need to answer each one. Choose those that most resonate with you and that most stretch you, and respond to those. The ones you choose should make you think about new things or in ways you haven't thought before.

Prospective Writing

Over the next six days, take each one of the *Six Fundamental Human Desires* and write down how this experience of lost innocence has opened news ways to think about that desire and how you will use it for good going forward.

Find a time and place where you won't be disturbed. Write continuously for at least fifteen to twenty minutes. Don't worry about spelling, grammar, or punctuation. This isn't an English class. Write only for yourself. Use "I" statements and "insight words." Make the writing extremely intimate and personal. Don't dwell on what was; focus on what still can be.

Look for positive intention, meaning, how these desires can open new doors and expand your horizon. When you're done with your writing, create a constructive affirmation using the structure explained next.

"I may have lost _____ [fill in the blank with something that was meaningful], but I have found _____ [fill in with something that has new meaning]. And its gift is that _____ [fill in with how this can be used in the future].

Here is an example:

"I may have lost the belief that I can control everything in life if I just try hard enough or do the right thing, but I have found that when I embrace the unknown, I feel more unencumbered and freer to try new things. And its gift is that I will be more confident about taking healthy risks in the future."

What Dreams May Come

"Anticipatory savoring" is a technique that activates a positive experience in advance. Write down three good things that you anticipate coming out this experience with lost innocence and what you can do to make it more likely to happen. It may be something in the short-term, like seeing a new friend who you met because of this situation, or else in the distant future, for example a change in career or going back to school. In the spirit of grounded hope, it can also be helpful to write down three coping strategies, such as reaching out to a trusted friend, exercising, mindfulness techniques, in case that desired situation takes longer than expected or must change for some reason. You can also make alternative strategies so that good fruit still can be found.

Aspire to Inspire

We earlier talked about the *Three Cs of Self-Expression: Choose, Create*, and *Contribute*. Well, they are especially important now as you consider your story. Answer the following three questions:

1. Who must I *choose* to be because of this challenge or loss?

2. What must I do and *create* because of this challenge or loss?

3. What must I *contribute* to others and the world because of this challenge or loss?

This is a great time to consider your core beliefs and principles, passions and hobbies, rituals and practices, community and connections. Also, ask yourself how you will be accountable to these acts of self-expression?

Main Theme

Now that you've gotten the fullness of how lost innocence has impacted your life—both in what was lost and what was found—it's time to identify the main theme of your story because every good story has one. It's often thought that the main theme is the moral, but that's not the case. Your main theme should be a statement on the human condition that your experience embodies. For instance, when I consider my own because of the heart attacks, here's what I'd say . . .

"We all have a tear in our lives, a hole in the center of us, an incompleteness that makes us vulnerable to attacks on our spirit, but our spirit can never be broken; rather, it can only be lost sight of. Spirit is always there to support us, to breathe life into us, no matter what happens; we just need to hold onto it."

So, what now is the main theme of *your* story?

Craft a New Story for the Future

Now, we've come to the moment that all your good work has been building to—the moment when you get to retell your story from a coherent perspective. A few tips to get you started:

- ✢ Don't worry about length. If you're writing it out, use as much paper as you need. If you're typing, don't check the page number.

- ✢ It doesn't need to be finished in one sitting. You may wish to work on it over multiple sessions. And it's okay to rewrite it; in fact, that's exactly what you'll want to do, to really get it right. Trust me when I say it is worth the effort.

- ✢ Watch out for the Survivor, Victim, or Martyr making themselves known. If they do, you may want to go back and review some of your previous notes.

- ✢ If fear grabs hold of the pen (or keys), try some grounding techniques, and drop in and see what's bubbling up.

- ✢ This is not mandatory, but it can be helpful to read your story out loud. You can do that yourself or have a trusted friend or family member either listen to it or read it back to you. The process of hearing is an altogether different experience.

Now, from a structural perspective, consider the following when crafting your story:

- ✢ Write it in the third person. No, I'm not kidding. There is something incredibly valuable about distancing yourself a bit at this point from your story. Write as though you were writing a novel, with "she," "he" or "they." It may feel awkward at first, but stick with it. The flow will soon start.

✛ Make sure you are starting *before* the experience or event that caused your challenge or loss. You want to locate yourself in "the ordinary world," to quote the *Hero's Journey*. The story should show what your desires, urges, problems, successes, strengths, unique characteristics, even flaws were *before*. Then take the story to the events that precipitated it.

✛ Consider using "insight words" or "phrases," ones that tell something about how you saw—and see—the world. "Because of this, she believed . . . ," "The message he took away was . . . ," "What she came to see was that . . . ," "What he's been given now is the gift of . . . ," "What they're committed to now is. . . ."

✛ Write with benevolent honesty. You are not a victim who needs to be coddled. You are also a person who needs not to be judged and to be treated with compassion. There may be moments when you feel sadness or pain, even anger—and that's okay. Crafting this story is not an attempt to be immune to difficult feelings. *Honoring the Past* and *Transforming the Present* didn't make them all go away; you just learned how better to manage them. Allow yourself to drop into emotions as they come up, and if they're too much, or else if you're ready to move on, drop out. What's wonderful about all the work you've done is that you can now allow yourself to truly and safely feel the effects of this experience—the painful ones and the joyful ones. The intimacy and clarity this gives you is what will allow the words to flow on the page with an authenticity that might surprise you.

✣ Make sure not to end with "today." The story must include your future horizon—what you envision as you sail into tomorrow's sun.

✣ When you've written the last word of your story, turn the page to a blank one and at the top put "Next Chapter"; then "...." Sometime when your new future becomes the past, you can record that here.

Once you've finished crafting your story and have reread it and are satisfied that the narrative feels *right* and *real*, take a moment to hold onto some air. Choose one of your favorite breathing exercises and sit with all the amazing work you've done. I don't say this lightly. If you have really gone through the HTC process fully; if you've taken the time to really consider and engage the exercises, it's a bit of a big deal. I firmly believe that anyone who has had a meaningful loss or challenge that has stolen a bit (or a lot) of their innocence is up to the challenge; moreover, that what they will gain from it will have led—and will continue leading—them to a more coherent, satisfying, and healthy life.

Lastly, we discussed how it takes roughly thirty days for the brain to rewire itself and for new patterns to take hold. So, it goes that for this story to really take root, it's a good idea to keep integrating it. For the next month or so, take time to reread your story—and not just the words, at a cognitive level; read it with your senses. Each time you do, drop into the emotions and sensations that bubble up. Really open up to what your spirit is communicating to your body.

RITUALS TO *CRAFT A NEW STORY FOR THE FUTURE*

The following rituals represent just a few possibilities for honoring all your work and experience. Use them only if they feel right. What's important is that you find a way to mark these efforts so that they feel meaningful to you. Maybe it's going to a place you find sacred; or making an offering of thanks; or listening to a particular song or reading some passage that embodies the main theme of your story. Maybe it's simply getting a confetti gun and shooting it off in the air. The sky's the limit! And it's yours to inhabit.

Let Go, Let Be Meditation

Set aside some quiet time free from distraction or interruption. Make sure wherever you are the temperature and light are comfortable. If you're indoors, adjust as necessary. Get into position; you can sit or lie down. Don't worry about maintaining any specific posture, simply allow yourself to relax into place.

Now it's time to start. Let yourself go . . . and let yourself be. Close your eyes slowly and start to ease your body. Gently breathe in. And gently breathe out. Allow all the tension from the process to slowly fall away. Feel the muscles in your body begin to give way. Allow your feet to get loose and heavy. Let your ankles drop toward the floor. Feel your calves and thighs getting limp; your hips and pelvis drawing downward. Let your stomach and back relax from all the stress they have been carrying. Feel your arms growing longer. Feel your shoulders fall. Allow your jaw to drop and your eyes to droop.

Next, focus on your breath. Breathe in through your nose and out through your mouth. Move the air slowly, evenly, deeply. Feel yourself aligning with the natural flow of life. As you do, feel the peace within begin to reveal itself. Feel yourself freer, calmer, and more at ease.

Now, turn your attention deeper within to the place that only you can go, to the center of your being, the home of your spirit. That sacred space beyond all your thoughts and skills. Beyond all your worries and concerns. Beyond all the drama and distraction, and all the sadness and suffering that has held you back and cloaked you in a veil. Feel the warmth, the light, the energy of authenticity pulsating in time with your heart.

You are not your fears. You are not the characters others may want you to play. You are a sacred self. An authentic being.

Journey now to this sacred center. Allow yourself to fall into it freely. As you breathe in and out, say the words, "I am." As you breathe out, say the words, "I can." In this inner sanctum, feel the warmth, the light, the energy of your spirit pulsing in time with your heart. Repeat the words, "Authentic being comes from authentic seeing."

Now, imagine yourself as a child. What dreams did you have? What were your hopes for your future self? As you breathe in, continue to say the words, "I am." As you breathe out, say the words, "I can."

Now, envision your future self, the one you wrote about in your story in all the detail you can create. Sit with this image for a few moments. As you become more and more present to it, feel its light and peace. Allow yourself to step into this image and become fully this person. Become who you have always been. Become who you are. Become who you can and will always be. Just for this moment, *be*. This is your coherent, authentic self.

When you're ready, pay attention to your breathing once again. And begin to come back into your body, holding onto the image of your coherent self. As you feel your muscles reawakening, and your body replenishing itself with energy, repeat the words, "Help me to feel as I am, think as I can, and live as I ought." Or if you prefer, "I promise to feel as I am, think as I can, and live as I ought."

Open your eyes slowly, feeling centered and renewed. Sit quietly for a moment, as you reacclimate to your surroundings. As you move forward with new life, take notice of that *you* shining through.

Ikebana, Way of the Flowers

Ikebana is the ancient Japanese art of flower arranging. It comes from the Japanese word *ike*, meaning "alive" or "arrange" and *bana* for "flower." Originally, the practice was used as offerings in Buddhist temples, but became formalized in the fifteenth or sixteenth century. More recently, Ikebana has become more secularized, displayed as art in people's homes. Still, it maintains its meditative associations. Creating an arrangement is meant to be done in silence, so that the designer can observe and contemplate the beauty of nature and how all of life fits together as an integrated whole. Ikebana is an intentional practice, not merely putting flowers in a vase; in fact, it's not about flowers at all. It's about the person who arranges them and their desire to create balance and beauty in the world.

The principles of Ikebana include minimalism, proportion, form, shape and line, humanity, and aesthetics. The container used is shallow. And there are three main types of flowers and branches used. The longest branch represents heaven. The medium branch represents human beings. And the shortest branch represents earth. Additional flowers or rocks can be used as well. Floral frogs (or little foam or glass bases) can be used to hold the flowers and branches in place. When choosing materials for your arrangement, keep in mind that it's less about a specific flower and more how the pieces work together to create one meaningful, integrated creation that uses its components to play with the idea of space (like we now do with time).

PLEDGE OF ACTION FOR
CRAFT A NEW STORY
FOR THE FUTURE

Crafting a New Story for the Future is an empowering experience. Like the other time frames, it might be tempting to say, "Yeah, great! Got it! I'm good." But even now, even with all the coherence you've brought to your story and life, it still can be easy to fall back into old patterns—which, again, is why it's helpful to make a commitment to positive action. Choose at least two actions, and practice consistently for thirty days. Feel free to add your own commitments to the ones listed.

❖ I will continue to look to the future with benevolent honesty and grounded hope.

❖ I will engage my imagination to develop new story lines for my life going forward. I will welcome new characters and remain open to alternative plot lines. If I ever get "writer's block" because something unexpected happened in my life (perhaps another loss of innocence), and it seems as though my story has reached an end, I will remind myself that although I can't control everything in life, I am still the author.

❖ I will remember that although my story will end one day, I can always influence how it lives on and with whom after I'm gone.

✛ When I am faced again with adversity or loss, I will also ask myself, "Where do I desire my story to go from here? What can the next chapter of my life to look like?"

✛ I will look to the *Seven Pillars of Resilience* that can best help me to continue writing my story.

Craft a New Story for the Future is what we do to make that final move from being lost in the dark of lost innocence to being found, having regained life's light. It's given us a way to fully become the hero of our story—not because we wished it to be or because we bent realities into fantasies; rather, because we integrated all our insights and kernels of truth from *Honor the Past* and seeds-turned-fruit and regained self-trust from *Transform the Present* and created a coherent narrative that is the *right* one and *real* one for us.

CHAPTER TEN

FORWARD INTO
NEW LIFE

When I was girl, my family had a lilac tree. It was small, apropos to our house, but its scent was colossal. Every day while it was in bloom, I'd stick my face in its redolent, purple blossoms and inhale with the fervor of an addict. Something about that smell sends my spirit light-years away, and yet perhaps because I associate it with a happy childhood, it's also grounding, like its roots.

When I bought my home in Newburyport all those years later, it was in the dead of winter and blanketed in snow. It was only when spring burst into a panoply of color that my own lilac tree was discovered. I picked a handful of blooms the night before my first heart attack. I remember standing in the kitchen at the new farmer's sink that I had lovingly chosen as part of a big remodel and arranged the blooms in a vase with the same care as a surgeon, thinking, *Wow, what an amazing life I have now.*

That vase was still on my bedroom's nightstand when I came home from the hospital two and a half weeks later, only it's beautiful blooms had turned to seed. And then, as the year mark approached, again, the tree in the yard burst into a riot of sweet-smelling bloom.

For everything there is a season . . . It is a simple yet profound truth.

As I kicked off year two post–heart attacks, the insight I had gleaned about my beloved home now feeling like the "Daddy Bear Chair" came into stark relief—so much so that at one point the following March, I realized that I was increasingly finding myself sad. It was like living in a time capsule with treasures from a lost dream. Not only did it not feel like building the future I was crafting, but also it felt more like lamenting the past, instead of honoring it. Even Newburyport, the small town where I lived, the place I had intentionally chosen to root in after years of chaotic transition, felt somehow claustrophobic.

In April of that second year, I found myself in the San Francisco Bay Area. Like its predecessor, that year also had its challenges; and I really needed a few days away. I had lived in the Bay Area at the turn of the millennium, and something about it was calling. It's funny how the significance of a present moment can sometimes be found only when you're looking back from the future. After a few days in the West's spectacular beauty—with its mountainous terrain, soaring coastlines, and genteel, rolling vineyards, I had a chance meeting while at dinner one night; and when I left, I found myself with a very appealing job offer.

Signs are everywhere if we pay attention—or else, if we pay attention, we make meaning from happenchance. Either way . . .

After signing the closing documents for the house in Newburyport two and a half years earlier and stepping across its threshold for the first time as proud homeowners, my ex-husband and I had walked back over that threshold to get some items out of the car; only, we shut the home's front door with the keys locked inside—both sets. I scurried around the property, checking all the windows and doors. Also locked. Two hours and $150 for a lock-smith later and we were back inside.

I thought about this happenchance, as I contemplated whether to accept the new job, chuckling at the meaning of getting locked out of one's dream home on the first day of ownership. Leaving that home would certainly be the end of a chapter in my story, one that had I invested so much in crafting in every possible way. But I was also aware that there was still more of this story left to write, and with benevolent honesty I had to admit my main character needed a new setting.

The West has long been associated with hope and new begin-nings. From the Israelites crossing the Jordan River westward into the Promised Land, to Chinese Buddhism, which uses mov-ing West as a metaphor for enlightenment, to King Arthur's tales about travels west where a dynasty of Grail keepers resides, to American literature and lore that symbolizes the West with the pursuit of freedom and chasing audacious dreams. Then there is Shamanic wisdom that says that the West teaches us to release what is no longer useful in our lives. And so, in that spirit, I deter-mined to "cut the fat" and open the next chapter.

Within a month, the house was on the market; the furniture and belongings had been trimmed to only what was needed and desired; an older car was sold, so as not to have to ship it; cats had vet-approved documentation in preparation for the flight; and temporary housing in Marin (a beautiful mountainous area that connects the northern Bay Area to San Francisco via the Golden Gate Bridge) was secured, until something more permanent could be found.

One benefit of age is that you come to know yourself bet-ter; whether for good or ill, patterns emerge, and you find your-self saying more and more, "Oh yeah, I guess I *do* do that." One of those things that I apparently do is not vacillate once I make a big decision. In fact, it seems that once something shifts in me and I choose a path, there's no coming back. And I say that as a point of observation, not pride. Such was the case with the decision to move to the Bay Area. Still, when the time came, saying goodbye to that home and life was like any meaningful parting: poignant and with a dab or two of pain.

I got up early on the morning that I was to make my way west. I showered one last time beneath the showerhead I'd installed with my own hands. When I was dressed, I walked into my office that overlooked the farm and marshland, remembering all the times I had sat at my desk and watched my crane friend land and take flight. He was nowhere to be found at that moment, so I bid him a silent adieu. Before I went downstairs, I stepped into the guest bedroom and bathroom, admiring my handiwork with paint and fixtures there too. And then I stopped at the little bedroom that was once to be a child's room. A ripple of lingering sadness about the life that would never be swept over me.

My suitcases were waiting by the front door. As I made my way down to them, I took each tread as though it had a memory of its own. I paused at one point, recalling how many times they had collectively caught me when my blood pressure medication was too high, the world went suddenly black, and gravity pulled me tumbling down. When I reached the bottom, I took a final turn around the first floor—the living room, which I had painted the first night in my underwear; the sunroom, which my mother and I wallpapered while eating takeout cheeseburgers and Caesar salad, laughing as we argued which one of us was more anal about straight lines; the dining room that I wallpapered on my own one night, not stopping until the sun rose because the movers were coming the next day; the kitchen with all its renovated glory; the 1930s art deco light fixture that hung over the table, long-hunted and finally purchased from eBay; and finally, the small bathroom by the laundry room that once housed the Corian gorilla—before I had hoisted the beast out of its glue and dragged it kicking and screaming out the door and into the garage. So many memories in such a short time. And yet that short time felt like a lifetime.

How many lives do we live between birth and death? Are we even aware of when one starts and concludes? What makes one life distinct from another—a person, a place, a leaving, a coming? Perhaps they are not lives after all, separate and in situ; but rather seasons, as the "Good Book" tells us, that unfold into one another—the way chapters do in a coherent story. To be sure, I was leaving a house and a town and a state and a time zone, but as I boarded the plane and settled into my seat westbound, I was acutely aware that I wasn't leaving home; home was coming with me because the only place that home exists is deep within the eternal movement of our spirit.

FEELING "AT HOME" AND SAYING "HINENI"

There is a light within each of us that, when allowed to shine, will illuminate the world.

So often we walk along life's path more aware of the bright than our light. By "bright" I mean the successes or achievements that we are proud of or the "bling" of getting something we want. These are great to be sure, but they don't provide comfort or strength when adversity strikes. Only the enduring glow at the center of our being—the home of our spirit—can do that. And yet it's precisely when adversity strikes that our spirit starts to darken, and the home that we relied upon feels as though it's been hit by a category five hurricane. But while the body and mind may wither with time, our spirit never does. Even Hippocrates, Plutarch, Cicero, and Galen thought this is why people rally at the end of life because their spirit remains essentially intact and alight, even as the brain and body malfunction or decay.

Before my heart attacks, I wanted to live, more because I feared the alternative. But looking back, I can see that the alternative (death) was driving everything I was doing. Even when things were going well, this fear had me living a disjointed life: life *or* death; happy *or* sad; past *or* present *or* future; body *or* mind *or* spirit; using my energy to try to make up for lost time; trying to squeeze all my dreams and ambitions into whatever time there was; trying to plan for any and every eventuality; always feeling like I was living in a piece of a time and place. One can live a piecemeal, incoherent life without having it threaten their happiness or security; but the tension it causes lives just below the surface, waiting for a moment of crisis to erupt, to a colossally dislocating effect.

In the wake of my heart attacks, and after working through HTC, I came to see time much differently—perhaps like many whose experiences have threatened to extinguish it. Time is not a villain to fear or an enemy to conquer, but rather a partner to live with, move with, and trust. Although I acknowledge that time as we live it here on earth is a succession of moments and changes, I now see that there is a unifying continuum that endures throughout each one. Locating ourselves on that continuum generally, rather than in a single moment or single change, gliding back and forth with ease, as is necessary and desired, is what true wholeness looks and feels like.

It would be easy to say that innocence keeps us whole and that losing it is what tears us apart. But as wisdom throughout time and across culture tells us, we *all* have a "tear" in our lives, a hole in the center of us, an incompleteness that makes us vulnerable to attacks on our spirit. And yet the stories of resilience that have come down through millennia show us also that our spirit can never be broken, rather only be lost sight of.

There are few things in life that we can count on with certainty; we live, we die, and along the way we lose parts of our innocence. As I said in the beginning of this book, lost innocence is the price we pay for life. But as I've discovered it, through both challenge and joy, it can also be our greatest return on investment.

The story of my heart attacks that I have shared throughout this book is not the one I expected, planned for, or pursued. It was certainly not the one I set out to write. But write it I did—and write it I am still doing—because, like life, this story is the only one I have, and no one other than me can author it with integrity. But more importantly, and why I incorporated it here ... This story is ultimately not about my heart attacks; neither is it about my life. It is about *all* our lives—about the human condition. It tells of a journey we all must take along the knife-edge of life to the very core of existence, where we come face-to-face with the existential "homelessness" that is lost innocence. Lost innocence is immune to a person's background or beliefs; it is also life's greatest equalizer because regardless of where we come from or what we hold as true, the unknowing, unsettledness, and stranger-in-a-strange-land experience it engenders is universally felt.

The ragged tear that caused my heart attacks was in the wall of my coronary artery. It was invisible to the naked eye, but still it was a literal hole inside me. And yet as that hole healed and my body recovered, another hole emerged, this one tearing at the heart of my spirit. In two ways, it seemed, this attack was trying to kill me: twice via my body; and failing that, using fear, it tried to suffocate my resilient spirit. And so wily was this attack, it knew just where to strike because this spirit of death had always been my greatest fear.

Since I was young, I was afraid of nothingness, the void, of losing my life before I had done my best work; and, on the flip side, of living an unfulfilled life, especially after wasting a bunch of time in my youth. Then, in its final tactical blow, as if to have maximum impact, it struck just as I settled into a very fulfilling life in the home that I had long desired. Ambling around in that uncertain darkness, which I suddenly found myself in post–heart attacks, I considered the attack to be a great evil, the villain in my dwindling narrative. But embarking on that "hero's journey," to *Honor the Past, Transform the Present,* and *Craft a New Story for the Future* made me realize that perhaps my heart attacks were actually one of my greatest gifts. Like Camus, I too "found in me an invincible summer," a place where I can never be attacked, no matter what my circumstance or what I confront or what I consider my limits to be. This is the place that is the home where my spirit resides.

HTC, with its focus on developing a coherent sense of time, took me from having a hole in my heart to being whole in spirit. Although some physical damage in my heart remains, its metaphorical counterpart remains intact.

I'm an ordinary person; yet what happened to me is extraordinary. Perhaps, given my age and otherwise health, it was even more extraordinary. As a health condition it is, as one doctor kindly put it, "exquisitely rare." Yet over the years I've seen how "extraordinary" circumstances happen to all of us or to those we love. I see it in everyone I know, having to do variously with health, relationships, career, finances, opportunities, hopes, dreams, and possibilities, as well as with innocent assumptions about how life "should" be. Everyone I meet says, "This should not have happened to you." But we all have something happen to us, each in our own way and often at a time we least expect. We are, all of us, in this life together, in the most absolute sense. So, as I have considered it, I now see how these rare and extraordinary circumstances all add up to what turns out to be quite ordinary. It is nothing less than the human condition.

My circumstance shone a very stark light on the nature of the unknown that lies at the heart of human life. We don't always know what or when. We don't always know how or why. We don't know what the future holds, and not even the experts can always provide the answers we crave. Yet we must live and live well.

Throughout the ages people have contemplated what it means to live a good life—including myself. The most profound response I can think of comes down to one word: *hineni* (pronounced *he-NEE-nee*), the Hebrew word that means, essentially, "I am here, and I am ready." Where that "here" was for me, or what that "ready" meant, was, at that moment, yet to be known.

As a friend and Rabbi once told me, to say "hineni" signals the moment when we situate our own life story within the larger story of life—past, present, and future. In this way, hineni is the definition of having a coherent sense of time. And we do this not merely with passive awareness, but with active commitment. Hineni embodies an open mind, a willing body, and an engaged spirit, even in the face of uncertainty or nothingness. It is a word that stands for light that cannot be drowned out by darkness. No matter how black or bright the hour, hineni. No matter how hopeless or hopeful we feel, hineni. We may quiver and waver and doubt for a time, but we are ultimately rooted, steadfast, and confident in our true home, hineni.

Whenever a character in the Hebrew Bible experienced a moment of meaningful crisis or change, they announced, "Hineni. Here I am." More than being physically present in a specific location, hineni is an existential expression of saying yes to life. Indeed, it is our response to life when it calls, even if that call is in the form of lost innocence. Judaism teaches that each person is responsible for their own prayer, just as the existentialists who say that everyone is responsible for their own life. In saying hineni, we are accepting that responsibility by rising fully from where we fell, when lost innocence pulled the rug out from our lives, and stepping forward into life, "all in," as my Rabbi-friend put it, and making *all* of ourselves available to every aspect of it.

AND SO, WE GO . . .

We've now come to the end of our journey together, having ventured down two very different paths: *Back and Blue* and *Lost and Found*. For any small loss, the first path works just fine. It asks us only to replace what we lost; we get new keys, replace a cell phone, shop for a new car, and so on. But when we lose a part of our innocence, we now see that it can never be replaced. As I said earlier:

> *We cannot re-create our lives going backward.*
> *We can only reclaim our life moving forward.*

Path One, *Back and Blue*, the path to nowhere, only prolongs our suffering because it keeps us stranded in that strange new world where everything is familiar, yet nothing seems the same. *Back and Blue* is cunning with its false promises of safety, security, and stability; of making us think that we can fill the hole in our heart by trying to go back "home"—back to happiness, wholeness, and peace. But the simple truth is that we can't go back.

Path Two, *Lost and Found*, the *Path of Resilience*, does not show us the way "back" home. Instead, it honors our pain, engages our spirit, and helps us move forward to create a new home. *Lost and Found* understands that things morph, places change; everything in life is in a constant state of transformation. It also acknowledges that home is not a place, person, or thing by itself; rather, it is that felt sense of coherence deep within our being that accompanies us everywhere we go.

I named this book *Holding onto Air* because grasping for the life we lost, as we do when we travel down *Back and Blue*, has the same success as trying to clutch the life-giving gas. But while our hands can't physically grip air, holding onto it and distributing it, through the process of breathing, is precisely what we do at every moment of our lives. In this way, the vital energy of our spirit is like air to our lungs; it fills us up, makes us come alive, and without it we die. Perhaps it is not a coincidence that *pneuma* the Greek word for "breath" is also the word for "spirit." Spirit is always there to support us, to breathe life into us, no matter what happens; we just need to hold onto it.

As you continue to move along life's path, always remember that we don't survive despite challenge and loss, we flourish *because of* them. We don't build resilience by focusing merely on "now," but rather by honoring and integrating all experience—past, present, and future—into the fullness of life and into the fullness of our being.

In the face of challenge and loss, especially the loss of innocence, will you allow yourself to become embittered or emboldened? Will you transform to triumph—renew, not retreat? Will you rise from ashes of chaos and loss, like the fabled phoenix, with life?" Will you say hineni?

This is your challenge and your choice.

MY "NEXT CHAPTER" . . .

I thought the Ides to beware were in March, not June.

June 13. Nearly ten years to the day after heart attack number one.

It was a glorious day in the San Francisco Bay Area. It was "seventy-two and sunny," as the saying goes, and I was cruising along Route 580 (or 880 or 680 or 80—I can never remember which is which), with the windows down and the sunroof open, singing along gayly with whatever music Spotify had randomly chosen for me. I was on my way to meet a dear friend and fellow SCAD survivor for lunch in central Marin, where she lived. It was just before noon, one of the few hours when the six-lane highway doesn't resemble a parking lot.

I remember nothing about the drive before IKEA. When the legendary yellow and blue of the building burst in front of the windshield, another coronary artery burst in my heart. For ten years I had been managing "shadow symptoms," those sensations that mimicked, albeit less severely, what I felt when I was having the earlier attacks. My personal constellation of symptoms was chest strain, back pain, and shortness of breath. When one snuck up, I monitored it without much concern. If two decided to tag team, I took it easy and watched them closely. If ever all three coincided, like they did with the second heart attack, I'd know the elephant was back, paying me a visit. Thankfully, he'd kept his distance for the last decade; but apparently, he missed me.

So, here's a dilemma: in that moment, when you're flying down the highway at seventy miles an hour and your chest is collapsing and you're struggling to breathe, do you pull over to the side of the road and dial 911—because if your heart gives out in one final blow and you suddenly become incapacitated, you could a) die from getting into an accident, presuming you're not already dead, and b) potentially injure others in a crash? Or alternatively, do you continue at mock speed, down another highway, over a long bridge that is notorious for traffic at odd hours, and up a long, curvy road where you know at the end is a hospital—because if you do pull over and call 911, it will take at least five or six minutes for the paramedics to get to you? And when they do get to you, they will almost certainly take you to a hospital of ill repute, where it's unlikely that they've even heard of SCAD, let alone would know what to do for it (trust me, not all of them do), because technically, that is the closest hospital.

It's a testament to the brain's awesomeness just how many thoughts it can process in the space of a few seconds. I remember thinking, in addition to everything just mentioned, *Well, given that the first time I had been having a heart attack for three days before going into the hospital, chances are that I could probably make it the twenty minutes it would take to get to the hospital of my choice. And given that I didn't die that time from a 'final blow,' maybe this time I wouldn't either.* I went with option number two.

I was grateful at that moment for having learned to drive in Boston, where the expression "Mass-hole" is a badge of honor for what we see as our assertiveness and agility on the road. I gassed the pedal, trying desperately to hold onto any and all air I could. When I finally saw the big, red cross and ER sign, I turned Dukes-of-Hazzard-like into the parking lot, up to the concierge stand, and, stumbling out, threw my keys at a poor, unsuspecting attendant who was calling, "Ma'am, can I help you?"

"I've had two heart attacks!" I said, trying to yell, but my lungs couldn't muster it. I choked out, "Ten years ago . . . SCAD . . . chest pain . . . back pain . . . can't breathe right . . . it's happening aga . . ."

"Wheelchair!" the attendant screamed, and within seconds I collapsed into a seat.

As I passed through the sliding glass doors, and a man in scrubs took over the steering, I closed my eyes, falling into the dark uncertainty that I had emerged from all those years before. *Three strikes, you're out! Body betrayed me . . . just like last time . . . can't be trusted . . . death all over again. I've had it . . . Can't do this again!*

Every part of me ached for the night before, when everything was just how it had been for the last decade: safe. And now here I was once more, walking on the knife-edge of life. The ER's fluorescent light overhead was garish and cold, mocking my fear, playing Tiddlywinks with my memories and thoughts, drowning out the warm light deep within. A few minutes later, like the previous times, oxygen tubes were secured onto my face, making it a little easier to breathe. The room—minutes before hustling with people taking blood from my arm, doing an EKG, making notes about medical history, asking about Advanced Directives and who should be called with the news—emptied. I dimmed the light as low as it would go. For a few moments, it was only me and the staccato from the heart monitor. My father's words came flooding back about making Mother Nature your friend. *How do I make her my friend, when she's trying to crush the life out of me—for a third fucking time!*

Hineni. The word tumbled into my mind, like a rock careening down a steep hill. No matter how black the hour, hineni. No matter how hopeless we feel, hineni. We may quiver and waver and doubt for a time, but we are ultimately rooted, steadfast, and confident in our true home, hineni.

For so long after my first two heart attacks, the last thing I wanted to do was feel my heartbeat because it was a reminder of all it—and we together—had been through. Not being able to feel its sensations, I took to mean that everything was still okay. But at that moment, I allowed myself to drop into my heart's rhythm. *Boom, boom . . . swish . . . Boom, boom . . . swish . . . Boom, boom . . . swish.* . . . Over and over. I found myself being lulled somewhere that was no longer garish and cold, but welcoming and warm. My breathing slowed, and with it, so too did the monitor's signal. Each beat no longer scared me, as it had the previous times. Right then, it felt like a reminder to my spirit that *I am here . . . still here.* Hineni.

I knew I was nowhere near being out of the woods—or even if I would see open skies again, but I took comfort in that eternal moment that at least I was still holding onto air.

And I still am . . .

GLOSSARY

Autonomic nervous system: An involuntary and reflexive, "behind-the-scenes" mechanism in our body that helps to keep us alive. Its job is to regulate how our internal organs function, including the heart, stomach, and intestines. The nervous system has two primary **branches:** the sympathetic nervous system, which mobilizes our body's internal resources against threats, and the parasympathetic nervous system, which keeps our body in a restorative and resting state.

Back and Blue: The path we naturally take when lost innocence strikes and we try to get back the life we once had. It's the path to "nowhere," keeping us in a dispiriting limbo.

Benevolent honesty: A clear-eyed, no-rose-colored glasses, no blinders, no exaggeration way to engage with challenge or loss, but doing so with kindness and compassion—an embodied gentleness with ourselves and others as we absorb new realities.

Centering: The internal process of anchoring our physical body; that is, getting into a relaxed and focused state by bringing calm to emotions.

Coherent sense of time: Being able to see ourselves *fully* in the past, present, and future, and holding each timeframe with equal value and importance.

Dynamic balance: Holding contradiction and uncertainty; moving with the forces of life; finding stability amid chaos or change with quiet, intentional surrender.

Embodied state (embodiment): Being aware of our thoughts, feelings, emotions, and bodily sensations.

Emotions: Complex reaction patterns, brought on by neurophysiological changes, variously associated with feelings, thoughts, and behavioral responses; inherently neither good nor bad, they're simply messengers.

Fear: A basic emotion that serves an adaptive function by protecting us from danger and helping us to react very quickly to threatening situations. A healthy amount of fear helps us survive; an unhealthy amount diminishes the quality of life.

Forgiveness: The intentional release of feelings of resentment or vengeance toward a person or group who has harmed us. Forgiveness is concerned with an individual relationship and a specific offense.

Grace: That which has been kindly done for us; benevolent giving; feeling we're blessed (generally speaking) beyond what we might have reasonably expected.

Grounding: The process of strengthening your connection with and comfort in our physical environment or the earth.

Hineni: The Hebrew word meaning, "I am here, and I am ready." Hineni embodies an open mind, a willing body, and an engaged spirit, even in the face of uncertainty or nothingness. Hineni is an existential expression of saying yes to life.

HTC: The acronym for *Honor the Past, Transform the Present,* and *Craft a New Story for the Future*—the framework in this book for the *Path of Resilience: Lost and Found.*

Lost innocence: The universal experience of meaningful, disorienting loss—when the unimaginable strikes, of having your core beliefs and principles called into question and your certainty challenged, of feeling untethered from yourself, others, or the world.

Mindfulness: Maintaining a moment-by-moment awareness of our thoughts, feelings, bodily sensations, and surrounding environment, through a gentle, nurturing lens; helps to relocate ourselves in a safe and grounded present.

Moral injury: A transgression of conscience. It's what happens when a person's core moral foundations are violated in high stakes situations. This violation recasts the way people see themselves, others, and the world and causes changes in behavior that signal a loss of trust, connection, self-worth, and meaning.

Neuroscience: The study of how the nervous system develops, its structure, and what it does.

Reconciling: Making peace with and finding coherent meaning in our broader sense of self in relationship to others and the world after a loss, an affront, or injustice.

Resilience: The capacity to rally from life's trials and tribulations, strengthened by the circumstances, and better equipped to live fully, love deeply, and weather future crises with poise.

Self-mastery: The present-focused realization that we can always be in command of ourselves—body, mind, and spirit—even while accepting that we may not be able to control all situations or outcomes. It's about learning how to *struggle well* (see entry following).

***Seven Pillars of Resilience*:** What makes resilience possible. Capacities that buttress us during moments (or durations) of adversity. The seven presented here are: patience, meaning-making, love and connectedness, forgiveness and reconciling, self-expression, self-mastery, dynamic balance.

***Six Fundamental Human Desires*:** What we inherently and essentially long for to be happy and well: meaning, purpose, value, connection, resilience, and transcendence. More fulfilling than mere survival needs, but also more enduring and rooted than wants. Desires are energized and empowered by the potential for true joy, contentment, self-worth, and peace. They are our core; they directly motivate our spirit; and they sustain us in all circumstances throughout our lives.

Somatic psychology/therapy: A form of body-centered therapy that looks at the connection of mind and body and uses both psychotherapy and physical therapies for holistic healing.

Spirit: The animating energy at the core of our lives. Its expression can be, but does not have to be, dependent on an explicit belief system.

Struggle well: Being mindful of our feelings, thoughts, and deeds, so that in any moment, no matter how difficult, we can make an intentional choice to follow our own good sense and moral compass.

The Gray Life: A blunted, one-dimensional existence defined by scarcity, separation, and sacrifice that cuts us off from important aspects of who we are and from events or people that have shaped our lives.

Three Harmful Personas: Unhealthy ways that we respond to and act out when lost innocence strikes, causing us to become shells of who we were. They are the survivor, victim, and martyr.

Trauma: "What happens to a person where there is either too much too soon, too much for too long, or not enough for too long" (Stephen Porges). An event, circumstance, or experience resulting in harm: physically, emotionally, relationally, or spiritually.

Window of tolerance: The optimal physiological arousal level that allows emotions to ebb and flow.

REFERENCES

Abdullah, Yusuf Ali, and Tom Griffith. *The Holy Qur'an Paperback*. Wordsworth Editions Ltd, 5th ed., 2001.

Aftab, Awais, Ellen E. Lee, Federica Klaus, et al. "Meaning in Life and Its Relationship with Physical, Mental, and Cognitive Functioning." *Journal of Clinical Psychiatry* 81, no. 1 (2019). doi: 10.4088/jcp.19m13064.

Allen, Summer. (2019). "How thinking about the future makes life more meaningful." *Greater Good Magazine*. The Greater Good Science Center at the University of California, Berkeley, 2019. https://greatergood.berkeley.edu/article/item /how_thinking_about_the_future_makes_life_more_meaningful.

American Psychological Association. *The Road to Resilience*. Washington, DC: American Psychological Association, 2014. http://www.apa.org/helpcenter/road-resilience.aspx.

Antonovsky, Aaron. *Health, Stress, and Coping*. Hoboken: Jossey-Bass, 1979.

Antonovsky, Aaron. "The Sense of Coherence—An Historical and Future Perspective." *Journal of Medical Sciences* 32, no. 3–4 (1996b): 170–78.

Bailey, Ryan, and Jose Pico. "Defense Mechanisms." NIH National Library of Medicine and Treasure Island, FL: StatPearls, 2020. https://www.ncbi.nlm.nih.gov/books/NBK559106/.

Beck, A. T. "Thinking and Depression: I. Idiosyncratic Content and Cognitive Distortions." *Archives of General Psychiatry* 9, no. 4 (1963): 324–33.

Breazeale, Daniel, ed. *Nietzsche: Untimely Meditations*. Cambridge and New York: Cambridge University Press, 1997. https://doi.org/10.1017/CBO9780511812101.

Brown, Brené. *Braving the Wilderness: The Quest for True Belonging and the Courage to Stand Alone*. New York: Random House, 2017.

Campbell, Joseph. *The Hero's Journey*. Novato: New World Library, 2014.

Cardeña, E., and D. Spiegel. "Dissociative Reactions to the San Francisco Bay Area Earthquake of 1989." *American Journal of Psychiatry* 150, no. 3 (1993): 474–78. https://ajp. psychiatryonline.org/doi/abs/10.1176/ajp.150.3.474.

Chang, Larry. *Wisdom for the Soul: Five Millennia of Prescriptions for Spiritual Healing*. Washington, DC: Gnosophia Publishers, 2006.

Chapman, Benjamin P., Kevin Fiscella, Ichiro Kawachi, et al. "Emotion Suppression and Mortality Risk over a 12-Year Follow-up." *Journal of Psychosomatic Research* 75, no. 4 (2013): 381–85. https://doi.org/10.1016/j.jpsychores.2013.07.014.

Cohen. Randy, Chirag Bavishi, and Alan Rozanski. "Purpose in Life and Its Relationship to All-Cause Mortality and Cardiovascular Events: A Meta-Analysis." *Psychosomatic Medicine* 78, no. 2 (2016): 122–33. doi: 10.1097/PSY.0000000000000274.

Duggal, Devika, Amanda Sacks-Zimmerman, and Taylor Liberta. "The Impact of Hope and Resilience on Multiple Factors in Neurosurgical Patients." *Cureus* 8, no. 10 (2016): e849.

Eagleman, David. *Incognito: The Secret Lives of the Brain.* New York: Random House/Pantheon Books, 2011.

Einstein, Albert. From a statement to William Miller, as quoted in *LIFE* magazine. May 2, 1955.

Eisenberger, Naomi, and Matthew D. Lieberman. "Why Rejection Hurts: A Common Neural Alarm System for Physical and Social Pain." *TRENDS in Cognitive Sciences* 8, no. 7 (2004): 294–300.

Emerson, Ralph Waldo. *Self-Reliance: An Essay.* White Plains: Peter Pauper Press, 1967.

Existentialism. In *Stanford Encyclopedia of Philosophy online.* https://plato.stanford.edu /entries/existentialism/.

Farb, Norman A. S., Zindel V. Segal, and Adam K. Anderson. "Attentional Modulation of Primary Interoceptive and Exteroceptive Cortices." *Cerebral Cortex* 23, no. 1 (2013): 114–26. https://doi.org/10.1093/cercor/bhr385.

Fledman, David B., and Lee Daniel Kravetz. *Supersurvivors: The Surprising Link Between Suffering and Success.* New York: Harper Wave, 2015.

Fleming, John, and Robert J. Ledogar. "Resilience, an Evolving Concept: A Review of Literature Relevant to Aboriginal Research." *Pimatisiwin* 6, no. 2 (2008): 7–23. https:// pubmed.ncbi.nlm.nih.gov/20963184/.

Foy, David, Kent D. Drescher, and Patricia J. Watson (2011). "Religious and Spiritual Factors in Resilience." In *Resilience and Mental Health: Challenges Across the Lifespan*, edited by Steven M. Southwick, Brett T. Litz, Dennis Charney et al. Cambridge University Press, 2011, 90–102. https://doi.org/10.1017/CBO9780511994791.008.

Frankl, Victor. *Man's Search for Meaning.* New York: Simon & Schuster, 1984.

Frasure-Smith, N., F. Lespérance, and M. Talajic. "Depression Following Myocardial Infarction: Impact on 6-Month Survival." *Journal of the American Medical Association* 270, no. 15 (1993): 1819–25. https://pubmed.ncbi.nlm.nih.gov/8411525/.

Gaesser, Brendan, Kerri Keeler, and Liane Young. "Moral Imagination: Facilitating Prosocial Decision-Making through Scene Imagery and Theory of Mind." *Cognition* 171 (2018): 180–93. https://doi.org/10.1016/j.cognition.2017.11.004.

Gao, Feifei, Yuan Yao, Chengwen Yao, et al. "The mediating Role of Resilience and Self-Esteem between Negative Life Events and Positive Social Adjustment Among Left-Behind Adolescents in China: A Cross-Sectional Study." *BMC Psychiatry* 19, no. 1 (2019): 239.

Gendlin, Eugene T. *Focusing.* New York: Everest House, 1978.

Gerin, William, Matthew J. Zawadzki, Jos. F. Brosschot, et al. (2012). "Rumination as a Mediator of Chronic Stress Effects on Hypertension: A Causal Model." *International Journal of Hypertension* (2012): 453–65. https://doi.org/10.1155/2012/453465.

Glaser, Judith E. "Self-Expression: The Neuroscience of Co-creation." *Huffington Post*, December 6, 2017. https://www.huffpost.com/entry/self-expression-the-neuro _b_9221518.

Greenfield, Emily A. "Felt Obligation to Help Others as a Protective Factor against Losses in Psychological Well-Being Following Functional Decline in Middle and Later Life." *Journals of Gerontology: Series B* 64B, no. 6 (2009): 723–32. https://doi.org/10.1093/geronb /gbp074.

"Guillaume Apollinaire quotes," Qu*otes of Famous People.* https://quotepark.com/authors /guillaume-apollinaire/.

Harris, Sam. *Waking Up: A Guide to Spirituality Without Religion.* New York: Simon & Schuster, 2015.

Hershfield, Hal E., Daniel G. Goldstein, William F. Sharpe, et al. "Increasing Saving Behavior through Age-Progressed Renderings of the Future Self." *Journal of Marketing Research* 48 (2012): S23–S37. https://doi.org/10.1509/jmkr.48.SPL.S23.

Hershfield, Hal E., and S. J. Maglio. "When Does the Present End and the Future Begin?" *Journal of Experimental Psychology: General* 149, no. 4 (2020): 701–18. https://doi. org/10.1037/xge0000681.

Hollingdale, R. J., and Helen Zimmern. *Nietsche: Human, All Too Human.* Cambridge and New York: Cambridge University Press, 1996.

Jänig, W. "Autonomic Nervous System." In *Human Physiology*, edited by R. F. Schmidt and G. Thews G. Berlin and Heidelberg: Springer, 1989. https://doi .org/10.1007/978-3-642-73831-9_16.

Jiang, Wei, and Jonathan R. T. Davidson. "Antidepressant Therapy in Patients with Ischemic Heart Disease." *American Heart Journal* 150, no. 5 (2005): 871–81. https://doi .org/10.1016/j.ahj.2005.01.041.

Killingsworth, Matthew A., and Daniel T. Gilbert. "A Wandering Mind Is an Unhappy Mind." *Science* 330, no. 6006 (2010): 932. https://www.science.org/doi/10.1126 /science.1192439.

Knill, Paolo J., Ellen G. Levine, and Stephen K. Levine. *Principles and Practice of Expressive Arts Therapy: Toward a Therapeutic Aesthetics.* London: Jessica Kingsley Publishers, 2004.

Krauss, Ruth. *Open House for Butterflies.* New York: HarperCollins, 2001.

Laozi. *Tao Te Ching.* New York: Vintage Books, 1972.

Lieberman, Matthew D. *Social: Why Our Brains Are Wired to Connect.* New York: Crown Publishers, 2013.

Love, Shayla. "How Long Is Right Now?" *Wu Tsai Neuroscience Institute*, Stanford University, 2019. https://neuroscience.stanford.edu/news/how-long-right-now.

Marsh, Jason. "Why Mindfulness Matters." *Greater Good Magazine.* University of California, Berkeley, 2010. https://greatergood.berkeley.edu/article/item/ why_mindfulness_matters.

Maslow, A. H. "A Theory of Human Motivation." *Psychological Review* 50, no. 4 (1943): 370–96. https://doi.org/10.1037/h0054346.

Masten A. S. "Ordinary Magic: Resilience Processes in Development." *American Psychologist* 56, no. 3 (2001): 227–38.

May, Herbert G., and Bruce M. Metzger, ed. *The New Oxford Annotated Bible with the Apocrypha: Revised Standard Version, Containing the Second Edition of the New Testament and an Expanded Edition of the Apocrypha.* Oxford: Oxford University Press, 1977.

Moore, T. "Spirit, Soul, and the Secular: An Interview with Thomas Moore." *ScienceDaily*. Mount Sinai Medical Center, March 6, 2015. www.sciencedaily.com /releases/2015/03/150306132538.htm.

Murphy, Jeffrie G. *Getting Even: Forgiveness and Its Limits*. Oxford and New York: Oxford University Press, 2010.

Newman, R. "APA's Resilience Initiative." *Professional Psychology: Research and Practice* 36, no. 3 (2005): 227–29. https://doi.org/10.1037/0735-7028.36.3.227.

Noyes, Russell, Jr., and Roy Kletti. "Depersonalization in Response to Life-Threatening Danger." *Comprehensive Psychiatry* 18, no. 4 (1977): 375–84. https://doi .org/10.1016/0010-440X(77)90010-4.

Oettingen, Gabrielle, and Thomas A. Wadden. "Expectation, Fantasy, and Weight Loss: Is the Impact of Positive Thinking Always Positive?" *Cognitive Therapy and Research* 15, no. 2 (1991): 167–75. https://doi.org/10.1007/BF01173206.

Ogden, Pat. (2009). "Modulation, Mindfulness, and Movement in the Treatment of Trauma-Related Depression." *Clinical Pearls of Wisdom: 21 Therapists Offer Their Key Insights*, edited by M. Kerman, 1–13. W. W. Norton & Company, 2010.

Park, C. L., and M. C. Kennedy. "Meaning Violation and Restoration Following Trauma: Conceptual Overview and Clinical Implications." In *Reconstructing Meaning after Trauma*, edited by E. M. Altmaier, 17–27. Cambridge: Academic Press, 2017.

Poulin, Michael J., Stephanie L. Brown, Amanda Dillard, et al. "Giving to Others and the Association between Stress and Mortality." *American Journal of Public Health* 103, no. 9 (2013): 1649–55.

Prochazkova, E., and M. E. Kret. "Connecting Minds and Sharing Emotions through Mimicry: A Neurocognitive Model of Emotional Contagion." *Neuroscience & Biobehavioral Reviews* 80 (2017): 99–114. https://doi.org/10.1016/j.neubiorev.2017.05.013.

Ring, Patrick, and Christian Kaernbach. "Sensitivity Towards Fear of Electric Shock in Passive Threat Situations." *PLoS ONE*, 10(3) (2015). https://doi.org/10.1371/journal .pone.0120989.

Shalev, A. Y., T. Peri, L. Canetti, et al. "Predictors of PTSD in Injured Trauma Survivors: A Prospective Study." *American Journal of Psychiatry* 153, no. 2 (1996): 219–25. https://doi .org/10.1176/ajp.153.2.219.

Shankaracharya. Vedanta, E. W., see chapter 4, under Gnyana-Yoga, 73–74.

Sheng-yan. *The Six Paramitas: Perfections of the Budhisattva Path, a Commentary*. Dharma Drum, 2002.

Southwick, Steven M., George A. Bonanno, Ann S. Masten, et al. "Resilience Definitions, Theory, and Challenges: Interdisciplinary Perspectives." *European Journal of Psychotraumatology* 5, no. 10 (2014): 3402. https://doi.org/10.3402/ejpt.v5.25338.

Sue Monk Kidd Quotes. *Brainyquote.com*. https://www.brainyquote.com/quotes /sue_monk_kidd_505181.

Suttie, Jill. "Five Ways Mindfulness Meditation Is Good for Your Health." *Greater Good Magazine*. University of California, Berkeley, 2018. https://greatergood.berkeley.edu /article/item/five_ways_mindfulness_meditation_is_good_for_your_health.

Suttie, Jill, and Jason Marsh. "5 Ways Giving Is Good for You." *Greater Good Magazine*. University of California, Berkeley, 2010. https://greatergood.berkeley.edu/article /item/5_ways_giving_is_good_for_you.

Terr, L. C. "Childhood Traumas." In *Psychotraumatology*, edited by G. S. Everly and J. M. Lating, 301–20. Boston: Springer, 1995. https://doi.org/10.1007/978-1-4899-1034-9_18.

Townsend, Sarah S. M., Heejung S. Kim, and Batja Mesquita. "Are You Feeling What I'm Feeling? Emotional Similarity Buffers Stress." *Social Psychological and Personality Science* 5, no. 5 (2014): 526–33.

Tulku, Tarthanh. *Love of Knowledge*. Berkeley: Dharma Publishing, 1987.

Underhill, Evelyn. *Mysticism: A Study in the Nature and Development of Human Spiritual Consciousness, Mystical Theology, Visions and the Soul*, 12th ed., Adansonia Publishing, 2018 [1911].

University of California, Los Angeles. "Rejection Really Hurts, UCLA Psychologists Find." *Science News*, October 10, 2003. www.sciencedaily.com/releases/2003/10/031010074045. htm.

Van der Kolk, Bessel. *The Body Keeps the Score: Brain, Mind, and Body in the Healing of Trauma*. New York: Viking Press, 2014.

Vohs, K. D., B. D. Glass, W. T. Maddox, et al. "Ego Depletion Is Not Just Fatigue: Evidence from a Total Sleep Deprivation Experiment." *Social Psychological and Personality Science* 2, no. 2 (2010): 166.

Wade, N., J. M. Schultz, and M. Schenkenfelder, "Forgiveness Therapy in the Reconstruction of Meaning Following Interpersonal Trauma." In *Reconstructing Meaning After Trauma*, edited by E. M. Altmaier, 69–81. Cambridge: Academic Press, 2017. https:// doi.org/10.1016/B978-0-12-803015-8.00005-X.

Wegner, D. M., D. J. Schneider, S. R. Carter, et al. "Paradoxical Effects of Thought Suppression." *Journal of Personality and Social Psychology* 53, no. 1 (1987): 5–13. https://doi. org/10.1037/0022-3514.53.1.5.

Wiesel, Eli. *Night*. Paris, Les Editions de Minuit, 1958.

Wittmann, M. "Embodied Time: The Experience of Time, the Body, and the Self." In *Subjective Time: The Philosophy, Psychology, and Neuroscience of Temporality*, edited by V. Arstila and D. Lloyd, 507–23. Cambridge: MIT Press, 2014.

Worthington, Everett L., Jr. "The New Science of Forgiveness." *Greater Good Magazine*. University of California, Berkeley, 2004. https://greatergood.berkeley.edu/article/item /the_new_science_of_forgiveness.

Zimbardo, Philip, and John Boyd. "Putting Time in Perspective: A Valid Reliable Individual Differences Metric." *Journal of Personality and Social Psychology* 77 (1999): 1271–88. https://doi.org/10.1037/0022-3514.77.6.1271.

Zimbardo, Philip, and John Boyd. *The Time Paradox: The New Psychology of Time that Will Change Your Life*. Glencoe: The Free Press, 2008.

Zimbardo, Philip, Richard Sword, and Rosemary Sword. *The Time Cure: Overcoming PTSD with the New Psychology of Time Perspective Therapy*. Hoboken: Jossey-Bass, 2012.

FURTHER READING

Frankl, Victor. E. *Man's Search for Meaning: An Introduction to Logotherapy*. New York: Simon & Schuster, 1984.

Henderson, Michael. *Forgiveness: Breaking the Chain of Hate*. West Hartford: Book Partners, 1999.

Kabat-Zinn, Jon. *Wherever You Go, There You Are*. New York: Hyperion Books, 2009.

Kabat-Zinn, Jon. *Full Catastrophe Living: Using the Wisdom of Your Body and Mind to Face Stress, Pain, and Illness*. New York: Bantam Books, 2013.

Katie, Byron. *Loving What Is*. New York: Random House, 2003.

Kornfield, Jack. *The Art of Forgiveness, Lovingkindness, and Peace*. New York: Bantam Books, 2003.

Kubo, Keiko, and Schrempp Erich. *Keiko's Ikebana: A Contemporary Approach to the Traditional Japanese Art of Flower Arranging*. Clarendon: Tuttle Publishing, 2012.

Luskin, Frederic. *Forgive for Good*. New York: HarperCollins, 2002.

Luskin, Frederic. *Forgive for Love*. New York: HarperCollins, 2007.

Martin, William. *The Tao of Forgiveness*. New York: Penguin, 2010.

May, Rollo. *The Courage to Create*. New York: Norton, 1973.

Miller, D. Patrick. *A Little Book of Forgiveness: Challenges and Meditations for Anyone with Something to Forgive*. Berkeley: Fearless Books, 2004.

Moore, Thomas. *Care of the Soul: A Guide for Cultivating Depth and Sacredness in Everyday Life*. New York: HarperCollins, 1992.

Moore, Thomas. *Soul Mates: Honoring the Mysteries of Love and Relationships*. New York: Harper/Perennial Library, 1994.

Nhat Hanh, Thich. *Peace Is Every Step: The Path of Mindfulness in Everyday Life.* New York: Bantam Books, 1992.

Tutu, Desmond. *No Future Without Forgiveness.* New York: Doubleday, 2000.

Tutu, Desmond, Douglas C. Abrams, and Mpho A. Tutu. *The Book of Forgiving: The Fourfold Path for Healing Ourselves and Our World.* New York: HarperOne, 2014.

Wiesenthal, Simon. *The Sunflower: On the Possibilities and Limits of Forgiveness.* New York: Schocken Books, 1997.

GET HELP

If you are in crisis and in need urgent of help, reach out to these organizations:

National Suicide Prevention Lifeline
Call: 1-800-273-8255
Crisis Text Line: Text HELLO to 741741

Crisis counselors are available twenty-four hours a day, seven days a week. If the situation is potentially life-threatening, call 911 or go to a hospital emergency room immediately.

Grieving.com: A forum for people to connect with others and share stories of loss and healing. The forum has more than 45,000 active members and features topics ranging from terminal illness and sudden death to the loss of a pet. See forums.grieving.com.

Modern Loss: A hub for all aspects of loss: the taboo, hilarious, and unexpectedly beautiful terrain of navigating life after a death. They have great essays and guest posts. Find them at modernloss .com.

MISS Foundation: A volunteer-run nonprofit organization that supports people of all ages through the process of grieving the death of a child. They offer discussion forums, educational resources, biannual conferences, and local support groups, and grieving visitors can connect with a HOPE (Helping Other Parents Endure) mentor for individualized support. Find them at miss children.org.

The Compassionate Friends: A nationwide nonprofit organization that also supports and offers resources to families who are coping with the death of a child. In addition to its wealth of information about healing grief, TCF holds national and regional conferences, facilitates online and in-person support groups for grieving families, and broadcasts a weekly web radio series. Find them at compassionatefriends.org.

The Dougy Center provides a safe place for children, teens, young adults, and their families who are grieving a death to share their experiences. They offer peer support groups, education, and training. Visit dougy.org.

National Alliance for Grieving Children: The National Alliance for Grieving Children is a nationwide platform that connects professionals, consumers, and volunteers whose mission is to support children and teens through the grieving process. NAGC offers online education, a searchable support group database, and hosts an annual symposium about child grief. See childrengrieve.org.

Our Side of Suicide: A hub for those seeking hope, comfort, and support in the wake of suicide. Started by two women who met through a support group after losing their fathers to suicide. Both had the desire to elevate the discussion about suicide in an attempt to give a voice to those seeking encouragement. See oursideof suicide.com.

The Tragedy Assistance Program for Survivors (TAPS): A national nonprofit that offers compassionate care to all those grieving the loss of a military loved one. Find them at taps.org.

Concerns of Police Survivors, Inc. (COPS): A nationwide nonprofit 501(c)(3) organization that provides resources to assist in rebuilding the lives of the survivors of law enforcement officers killed in the line of duty, as determined by federal government criteria. Visit nationalcops.org.

The National Organization of Parents of Murdered Children: Provides ongoing emotional support, education, prevention, advocacy, and awareness for parents and families. Find them at pomc .com.

The Shay Moral Injury Center: Offers research, educational/ training programs for the public and service providers about the trauma of moral injury, and supports healing that enhances moral resilience. Find them at voa.org/moral-injury-center.

ACKNOWLEDGMENTS

To...

My indefatigable agent, Kimberly Cameron, whose fine taste in books is surpassed only by her fine taste in Bordeaux. Cheers! And the deepest bow of gratitude for *everything*.

Editors extraordinaire, Charlotte Ashlock and Jeevan Sivasubramaniam—whose apparent chutzpah in one of the "most heated pub meetings at BK" won the day. You have my eternal thanks and respect.

The nicest and most generously spirited book production team any author could dream of. This process was so damn fun! And special shoutout to my new best friend and brilliant cover-design-compatriot, Ashley Ingram. The planets are moving... we need to talk.

My dearest "sisters": SCAD sister, Heather Hawkins; Heart Sister, Erin Byrne; and Soul Sister Becca Adler. Words escape me when I think how much you mean to me.

"Mr. Funny"... because you know funny — and for seeing and nurturing my "spark" early on when it had all but eclipsed me. Without it, I doubt I'd have had the "courage to be"—and become.

My MacGyver... for keeping life's wolves away from the door, finding water in the mountains when we had none (you *such* the man!), letting me be endlessly silly, and continuing to flash that crooked, heart-melting smile through dark nights and bright days.

My parents ... you got the dedication, but it bears repeating: I would not be here without you—and not just because you gave me life. No daughter could be more grateful for all you are and all you've given me.

Con amore...

INDEX

ABOUT THE AUTHOR

Dr. Michele DeMarco is an award-winning writer and a specialist in the fields of psychology, trauma, health, and spirituality. She is also a professionally trained therapist, clinical ethicist, and researcher who's spent the last two decades studying trauma generally, moral injury and lost innocence specifically, and resilience. She is one of *Medium's Top Writer's for Mental Health and Health*, respectively, and the author of the *Psychology Today* blog: "*Soul Console: Healing from Moral Injury.*"

Michele's writing has appeared in national and international publications, including the *New York Times, POLITICO, The Boston Globe, The Daily News, Psychology Today, The War Horse, Forge, Elemental,* and *One Zero.* She has been featured as a psychology and spirituality expert for *MindBodyGreen, The Daily News, Integrative Practitioner, Lifehacker,* Bloomberg/WNBP Radio, and Partners HealthCare. Her upcoming novel, *About Others,* won the national

Mystery Writers of America's Helen McCloy Award for Mystery Writing. She's taught Creative Nonfiction and Conflict Transformation at California Institute of Integral Studies.

Dr. DeMarco's research spans the fields of moral injury, psychology, trauma, neuroscience, and somatic and creative art therapies, respectively, and world wisdom and spirituality. Out of this research, she has developed a writing therapy specifically for moral injury called Embodied Disclosure Therapy (EDT).

Michele lives in the San Francisco Bay Area with her partner, Andrew, and their Main Coon cat, Sophie.

Find Dr. DeMarco at micheledemarco.com.

Berrett–Koehler
Publishers

Berrett-Koehler is an independent publisher dedicated to an ambitious mission: *Connecting people and ideas to create a world that works for all.*

Our publications span many formats, including print, digital, audio, and video. We also offer online resources, training, and gatherings. And we will continue expanding our products and services to advance our mission.

We believe that the solutions to the world's problems will come from all of us, working at all levels: in our society, in our organizations, and in our own lives. Our publications and resources offer pathways to creating a more just, equitable, and sustainable society. They help people make their organizations more humane, democratic, diverse, and effective (and we don't think there's any contradiction there). And they guide people in creating positive change in their own lives and aligning their personal practices with their aspirations for a better world.

And we strive to practice what we preach through what we call "The BK Way." At the core of this approach is *stewardship,* a deep sense of responsibility to administer the company for the benefit of all of our stakeholder groups, including authors, customers, employees, investors, service providers, sales partners, and the communities and environment around us. Everything we do is built around stewardship and our other core values of *quality, partnership, inclusion,* and *sustainability.*

This is why Berrett-Koehler is the first book publishing company to be both a B Corporation (a rigorous certification) and a benefit corporation (a for-profit legal status), which together require us to adhere to the highest standards for corporate, social, and environmental performance. And it is why we have instituted many pioneering practices (which you can learn about at www.bkconnection.com), including the Berrett-Koehler Constitution, the Bill of Rights and Responsibilities for BK Authors, and our unique Author Days.

We are grateful to our readers, authors, and other friends who are supporting our mission. We ask you to share with us examples of how BK publications and resources are making a difference in your lives, organizations, and communities at www.bkconnection.com/impact.

Dear reader,

Thank you for picking up this book and welcome to the worldwide BK community! You're joining a special group of people who have come together to create positive change in their lives, organizations, and communities.

What's BK all about?

Our mission is to connect people and ideas to create a world that works for all.

Why? Our communities, organizations, and lives get bogged down by old paradigms of self-interest, exclusion, hierarchy, and privilege. But we believe that can change. That's why we seek the leading experts on these challenges—and share their actionable ideas with you.

A welcome gift

To help you get started, we'd like to offer you a **free copy** of one of our bestselling ebooks:

www.bkconnection.com/welcome

When you claim your **free ebook**, you'll also be subscribed to our blog.

Our freshest insights

Access the best new tools and ideas for leaders at all levels on our blog at ideas.bkconnection.com.

Sincerely,

Your friends at Berrett-Koehler